mustsees
Brussels

Museum of Musical Instruments/©Marcel Vanhulst/visitbrussels.be

mustsees **Brussels**

Editorial Manager	Jonathan P. Gilbert
Editor	M. Linda Lee
Writer	Kimberley Lovato
Production Manager	Natasha G. George
Cartography	John Dear
Photo Editor	Yoshimi Kanazawa
Photo Research	Sean Sachon
Layout	Chris Bell, cbdesign, Natasha G. George
Interior Design	Chris Bell, cbdesign
Cover Design	Chris Bell, cbdesign, Natasha G. George

Contact Us

Michelin Travel and Lifestyle
One Parkway South
Greenville, SC 29615
USA
www.michelintravel.com
michelin.guides@usmichelin.com

Michelin TravelPartner
Hannay House
39 Clarendon Road
Watford, Herts WD17 1JA
UK
(01923) 205 240
www.ViaMichelin.com
travelpubsales@uk.michelin.com

Special Sales

For information regarding bulk sales, customized
editions and premium sales, please contact
our Customer Service Departments:

USA	1-800-432-6277
UK	(01923) 205 240
Canada	1-800-361-8236

Michelin Apa Publications Ltd

58 Borough High Street, London SE1 1XF, United Kingdom

© 2012 Michelin Apa Publications Ltd
ISBN 978-1-907099-74-8
Printed: December 2011
Printed and bound: Himmer, Germany

Note to the reader:
While every effort is made to ensure that all information printed in this guide is correct and
up to date, Michelin Apa Publications Ltd. accepts no liability for any direct, indirect, or
consequential losses howsoever caused so far as such can be excluded by law. Admission
prices listed for sights in this guide are for a single adult, unless otherwise specified.

Grand Place

Introduction

TABLE OF CONTENTS

★★★ ATTRACTIONS

Unmissable historic, cultural and natural sights

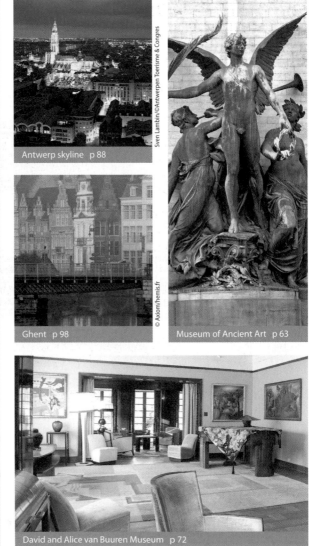

Antwerp skyline p 88

Sven Lambin/©Antwerpen Toerisme & Congres

Ghent p 98

© Axiom/hemis.fr

Museum of Ancient Art p 63

©Y. Duhamel/Michelin

David and Alice van Buuren Museum p 72

©Michel de Bray/Musée van Buuren

MUST KNOW

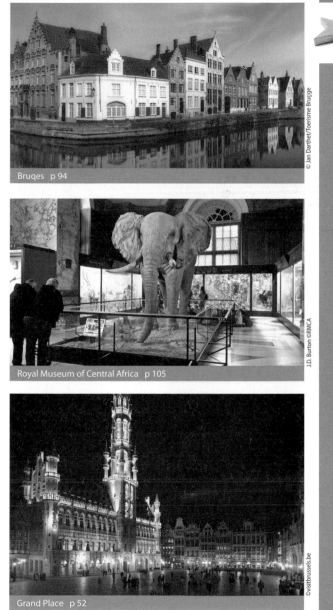

Bruges p 94

© Jan Darthet/Toerisme Brugge

Royal Museum of Central Africa p 105

J.D. Burton ©RMCA

Grand Place p 52

©visitbrussels.be

ACTIVITIES

Unmissable activities and entertainment

Le Chalet Robinson p 136

©Chalet Robinson

Tour a brewery p 74

©Brasserie Cantillon

Take the kids to Océade p 111

©Steven Richardson/visitbrussels.be

Hotel Metropole for a nightcap p 145

©Franck Duez/Hotel Metropole

Stroll Cinquantenaire Park p 85

©Julian Love/Apa Publications

Le Botanique p 117

©Hélène Dehon

Find solitude in Brussels Park p 84

©Olivier van de Kerchove/visitbrussels.be

Pantone Hotel p 149

©Sven Laurent/Pantone Hotel

★★★ ATTRACTIONS

Unmissable historic, cultural and natural sights

For more than 75 years, people have used Michelin stars to take the guesswork out of travel. Our star-rating system helps you make the best decision on where to go, what to do, and what to see.

★★★	Unmissable
★★	Worth a trip
★	Worth a detour
No star	Recommended

 # ACTIVITIES

Unmissable activities, entertainment, restaurants and hotels
**We recommend all of the activities in this guide, but our top picks
are highlighted with the Michelin Man logo.**

Outings
Art Nouveau Tour *p 14*
Brewery tour *p 68, p 74*
Brussels by bike *p 15*
Stroll Cinquantenaire
Park *p 85*
Take the kids to
Océade *p 111*

Hotels
Hotel Amigo *p 144*
Hotel Bloom *p 143*
Le Châtelain *p 148*
Odette En Ville *p 149*
Pantone Hotel *p 149*

Nightlife
Drinks at Winery *p 127*
Hotel Metropole for a
nightcap *p 145*
Jazz at L'Archiduc
p 126
Le Botanique *p 117*

Party on Place
St-Géry *p 55*
Puppets at Théâtre
Marionnettes de
Toone *p 118*

Relax
Find solitude in
Brussels Park *p 84*
Lunch on the Grand
Place *p 52*
Soak in the Thermal
Baths of Spa *p 107*

Restaurants
Belga Queen *p 133*
Comme Chez Soi *p 134*
Il Pasticcio *p 135*
La Mer du Nord *p 133*
Le Chalet Robinson *p 136*
Maison Antoine for
frites *p 135*
Toucan Brasserie *p 137*

Shopping
African fabrics *p 48*
Belgian Fashions *p 121*
Chocolates *p 124*
Christmas Market *p 19*
Edible souvenirs *p 123*
Flea market in Les
Marolles *p 121*
Sunday at Midi
Market *p 123*

Sports
Cheer on RSC
Anderlecht *p 115*
Formula 1 action *p 115*
Hike in the Sonian
Forest *p 84*
Ice skate *p 114*
Boat on the Mellaerts
Ponds *p 87*
Scuba dive *p 113*

STAR ATTRACTIONS

IDEAS AND TOURS

Throughout this thematic guide, you will find inspiration for a thousand different holidays in Brussels. The following is a selection of ideas to get you started. Sites in **bold** are listed in the Index.

Hit the Highlights

If this is your first time in the capital, there are things you just must see (you can always come back for the rest). Armed with curiosity and an intrepid spirit, you'll discover a city full of endless surprises.

◆ Everyone starts with the **Grand Place★★★**, and you should too. Here, you'll revel in what's often heralded as the most beautiful square in Europe.

◆ Wander through the **Galeries St-Hubert★★**, a 19C shopping arcade that conceals elegant shops, cafés and impressive architecture.

◆ Meet Tintin and his loveable dog, Snowy, among countless other characters, at the **Belgian Center for Comic Strip Art★★**.

◆ Ogle the work of Belgian surrealist painter René Magritte at the **Magritte Museum★★**, opened in 2009 and now the city's biggest cultural lure.

◆ Make a beeline for **Place du Sablon★**, where the best names in chocolate – **Pierre Marcolini** *(Rue des Minimes 1)* and **Wittamer** *(Place du Grand Sablon 13)* – melt in among the beautiful houses and restaurants.

◆ Check out the **Mont des Arts** area for its stellar views over the Lower Town, and visit the **Museum of Musical Instruments★★★**.

◆ Take a refreshing break at an outdoor terrace, perhaps in the lively **Place St-Géry**, and toast to Brussels with a Gueuze, Kriek or Faro beer, three local elixirs.

Design Your Own Tour

Grab a map from the **Brussels Info Point** (BIP) on the Place Royale, and hit the streets. The diverse neighborhoods of Brussels hide something to pique the interest of any traveler.

Comic Strip Trail

©J.P. Remy/visitbrussels.be

MUST KNOW

European Quarter

At first glance, most people get the impression that this Upper Town neighborhood consists only of nondescript office buildings, but hoof it around the European Quarter and you'll discover some worthwhile sites hiding between the cement and glass guardians. Stop by the lively square, **Place du Luxembourg**, a favorite of the after-work crowd that sits in the shadow of the **European Parliament**. You'll also find two well-known museums here, the **Wiertz Museum** and the **Museum of Natural Sciences★★**. Landscaped gardens and Art Nouveau architecture surround the adjoining squares, **Place Ambiorix** and **Place Marie-Louise**; nearby, the **Triumphal Arch** forms the entrance to **Cinquantenaire Park**.

Comic Strip Trail

Since 1991, the walls and gable ends of buildings in central Brussels have been animated with murals illustrating some of Belgium's best-loved comic strips. There are now more than 40 whimsical scenes depicting favorites like Tintin, Lucky Luke, Astérix and other jovial characters. Following the colorful 6km/3.7mi trail requires some endurance and comfortable shoes, but you won't be disappointed in Brussels' whimsical side. Pick up a detailed map at the Brussels Info Point (BIP) on Place Royale; or at the **Belgian Center for Comic Strip Art★★** *(Rue des Sables 20)*, a good place to start your tour.

To Market, To Market

See Shopping for a list of market days and locations.

René Magritte Museum

©Musée René Magritte, Jette-Brussels

Brussels is a city of neighborhoods, and there are dozens of markets every day of the week around the city. Whether you want to provision your own picnic, buy gifts to take home to your foodie friends, or simply ogle the produce and people-watch, going to the market is a favorite pastime in Brussels, and a great way to get to know the city.

Museum Mania

See Museums for details.
If you fancy famous artists, head for the **Magritte Museum★★** and the **Victor Horta House★★**. Looking to discover a lost art? Learn the intricacies of a Belgium art at the **Museum of Costume and Lace**; or seek hidden treasures in the **Ixelles Museum★★**. With more than 100 museums to choose from, museum maniacs will never run out of things to see in Brussels. For great discounts, make the museum rounds with a **Brussels Card** *(see Practical Information)*.

IDEAS AND TOURS

13

Guided Walking Tours

Arau
Boulevard Adolphe Max 55, Lower Town. Departure points vary. €10. 02 219 33 45. www.arau.org.
This respected company (whose name is an acronym for Atelier de Recherche et d'Action Urbaine) specializes in themed walking tours of Brussels, with an emphasis on Art Nouveau architecture. They also do an **Art Nouveau bus tour**; *departs from the Hotel Métropole on Place de Brouckère; €17).*

Be.Guided
Departure points vary. 04 955 38 163. www.beguided.be. Call or check online for rates. Spend a few relaxing hours walking through the heart of Brussels with enthusiastic guides who help you uncover the city's history, art and architecture, as well as the best food, drink and shopping.

Guides Brussels Belgium (GBB)
Tours depart from the Hôtel de Ville, on the Grand Place. 02 548 04 48. www.visitbrussels.be. Call or check online for rates.
Guided tours, on request, shed light on all aspects of Brussels, from architecture to the reign of Charles V. Experienced guides lead the way, providing narrative in a range of languages, including English. GBB also offers "No Reservation" guided tours *(English tour Sat 2pm; €10).*

Chocolate Tour
Tours depart from the Godiva shop on the Grand Place. Wed, Fri, Sat & Sun 9am. €69. Book online at www.city-discovery.com/brussels.
Learn the secrets of the wildly popular confection from master chocolatiers. On this four-hour walking tour, you'll taste your way through the best chocolate shops in the city center.

Bus Tours

Hop On, Hop Off
Book online or buy tickets at the tourist office at the Hôtel de Ville (Grand Place). €18. 02 513 89 40. www.viator.com.
Twenty-four-hour tickets allow you to catch a double-decker bus – one leaves every hour from the Gare Centrale (central train station; *Rue des Colonies 10)* – and get on and off at will at twelve locations around the city. Multilingual commentary imparts fascinating facts about Brussels.

Visit Brussels Line
Book online at www.city-discovery.com. €18.
Another hop-on, hop-off option, Brussels Line lets you explore the city at your own pace. Buses depart every hour from the Gare Centrale (central train station; *Rue des Colonies 10).*

Chocolate Tour

©Julian Love/Apa Publications

Bike Tours
Pro Velo

Most tours depart from the Cyclist's House, Rue de Londres 15, Ixelles. Metro: Trône. 02 502 73 55. www.provelo.org. Call for rates.

This company not only rents bikes, it also has built a reputation for guided weekend bike tours (*Apr–Sept*). Choose from 11 different city circuits, ranging from Brussels for Beginners to Beers and Breweries. Each tour lasts about four hours.

Boat Tour

©Rivertours

Boat Tours
Brussels by Water

Boulevard d'Ypres 84, Lower Town. Metro: Ribaucourt. Boats depart from Quai Béco (venue du Port) and Quai de Heembeek. Office open Mon–Fri 9am–12:30pm & 1pm–5pm. 02 218 54 10. www.rivertours.be.

From early May to late September, explore the Brussels region aboard a guided river cruise or a day trip on Belgium's canals. Combined boat and walking or biking tours are also available. Short cruises in Brussels start at €4.

Tour via Segway
Tours depart from the Hôtel de Ville, on the Grand Place. €39. 02 513 89 40. www.brussels-segwaytour.com.

Enjoy a new perspective on Brussels: from May through September, you can zip around the capital on a Segway to 17 different sites and monuments without wearing out your feet.

Go Green
The multitude of parks, gardens and forests in Brussels means that visitors will enjoy the greenest capital in Europe. The landscaped **Cambre Woods★** is the biggest park in Brussels, and it's closed to traffic on weekends. South of the city, **Sonian Forest★★** will please outdoorsy types year-round with trails for running, biking and cross-country skiing. Scope out a path on one of the trail maps posted at the forest entrances (*www.soignes-zonien.net*).

Quick Trips
Stuck for ideas? Try these:

IDEAS AND TOURS

CALENDAR OF EVENTS

From folklore festivals to edible events, Brussels keeps a year-round calendar of fun. Listed below is a selection of perennial favorite festivals. Dates and times vary; check event websites or www.visitbrussels.be in advance. Festivals are in Brussels, unless otherwise noted.

January

The Brussels Antiques & Fine Arts Fair
late January

Antiquities and other treasures arrive in Brussels each January at this, the largest antiques fair of its kind in Belgium. At the urban-chic Tour & Taxis building, 130 dealers sell quality pieces from furniture to African masks *(86c Avenue du Port; 02 513 48 31; www.brafa.be).*

February/March

Binche Carnival
early March

Each year during the four days preceding Lent, the medieval town of Binche *(62km/37mi south of Brussels)* hosts one of Europe's oldest surviving urban carnivals, which features hundreds of masked clowns called "the Gilles." This event has been recognized by UNESCO as a "masterpiece of intangible heritage of humanity" *(Caves Bette, Rue des Promenades 2, Binche; 06 433 67 27).*

April/May

Brussels International Fantastic Film Festival
mid-April

Vampires and ghouls and mummies – oh my! The stars of BIFF are creatures of the night. Screenings, competitions and "horrifying" happy hours are all part of the fun during this two-week festival held at Brussels' Tour & Taxis building *(86c Avenue du Port; 02 201 17 13; www.festivalfantastique.org).*

Royal Greenhouses of Laeken
mid-April–early May

For three weeks each spring, these stunning Art Nouveau glass structures are open to the public and reveal a collection of rare plants, super-sized flowers and lush foliage collected by King Léopold II. The evening sessions, when the iridescent 19C glass domes are lit from within, are particularly magical *(61 Domaine Royal, Avenue du Parc Royal; 02 513 89 40).*

Brussels Accessible Art Fair
mid-May & late October

High-quality, original contemporary artwork is offered to the public at affordable prices for three days in May and October. Started in 2006, the BAAF is now a major event on the city's

January: The Brussels Antiques & Fine Arts Fair

©BRAFA

cultural calendar, attracting thousands of art lovers *(Conrad Brussels Hotel, Avenue Louise 71; www.accessibleartfair.com).*

Brussels Jazz Marathon
last weekend in May
Nearly 700 artists from around the world draw jazz fans to Brussels in May, when indoor and outdoor stages are set up to host music around the capital, including on the Grand Place *(various locations in central Brussels; 02 456 04 84; www.brusselsjazzmarathon.be).*

Procession of the Holy Blood
40 days after Easter
Hailed by UNESCO for Its cultural significance, this procession takes place in Bruges on the Feast of the Ascension. The Basilica of the Holy Blood has a reliquary said to contain the Blood of Christ, and some 80,000 spectators come to watch the relic being paraded through the streets in a procession depicting biblical scenes *(Burg 15, Bruges; 05 033 67 92; www.holyblood.org).*

June/July
Battle of Waterloo
June 18
If you hear gunfire and horses' hooves on June 18, fear not – it's only the reenactment of Napoleon's famous battle in 1815 *(Waterloo Battlefield, Route du Lion 315, Waterloo; 02 285 19 12; www.waterloo1815.be).*

Couleur Café
last weekend in June
This popular, fun and funky music festival harmonizes a variety of genres and cultures with art expos, concerts, a world food kitchen and much more *(Tour & Taxis, Avenue du Port 86c; couleurcafe.be).*

May and October
Brussels Accessible Art Fair
©BAAF

Ommegang
first weekend in July
This festival on the Grand Place unfolds in front of spectators and the royal family, and re-creates Charles V's joyous entry into Brussels on June 2, 1549. Space is capped at 3,000 people, so book ahead at the Tourist Office *(02 513 89 40; www.visitbrussels.be).*

Brussels Beach
early July–early August
A beach in Brussels? During the month of July the Quai des Péniches becomes Brussels' hottest beach resort, with sand, tropical drinks, entertainment and even a few palm trees *(Quai des Péniches; www.bruxelleslesbains.be).*

Belgian National Day
July 21
No matter where you are in Belgium on July 21, celebration ensues, commemorating the day King Léopold I was sworn in as the first king of the Belgians in 1831. Take advantage of free entry to tourist attractions and royal venues all over Brussels.

Royal Palace Opening
July 22–mid-September
Belgium's royal family now lives in the palace in Laeken, but the

former royal residence in central Brussels opens its doors once a year to the public for free *(Place de Palais; www.monarchie.be).*

Festival of Ghent

mid- to late July

Six international festivals converge to create the perfect storm of a party for ten days in Ghent's medieval center. Nearly 1.5 million people come to see parades, jousts, fireworks, puppet busking, street theater and music *(Vooruit Arts Centre, Sint Pietersnieuwstraat 23; Ghent; 03 226 49 63; www.10daysoff.be).*

Strantwerpen

summer months

Sports and cultural activities, as well as sun loungers, bars and food stalls, abound on a stretch of sand set up on Antwerp's docks along the Schelde River in the trendy Het Eilandje (The Little Island) district *(Antwerp; www.perrier-strantwerpen.be).*

August/September

Meyboom

August 9

A procession of giant puppets and the planting of a *meyboom* (Dutch for Maypole) marks one of the oldest traditions in Belgium. It takes place on August 9, the feast day of St. Laurence *(corner of Rue du Marais and Rue des Sables; www.meyboom.be).*

Brussels Flower Carpet

early August

Every other year in August, close to a million begonia flowers are used to create a lovely 3,000sq ft patterned "carpet" in the center of the Grand Place – all arranged by hand *(www.flowercarpet.be).*

Belgian Grand Prix

late August

At the end of August, the quiet town of Spa *(140km/87mi southeast of Brussels)* is fueled by high-adrenaline action when the Belgian Grand Prix roars onto the Spa-Francorchamps race circuit *(Route du Circuit 38, Spa; www.formula1.com).*

Urban BBQ

late August

Not your average cookout, this event sees some of Belgium's best chefs take to their grills for a weekend. Visitors enjoy the results at communal tables set up on the esplanade in the Mont des Arts quarter *(02 375 96 08; www.urbanbbq.be).*

Brussels Flower Carpet

©Avi&Gulli, Gaston Batistini, Labo River, Michel Block/ www.flowercarpet.be

Beer Weekend
early September
More than 50 Belgian breweries set up their suds for tasting during this fall weekend *(Grand Place; 02 511 4987; www.belgianbeerweekend.be).*

Design September
September
This full month of activities, linked to contemporary design, features more than 30 events, workshops and open houses in and around the city *(various venues around Brussels; 02 349 35 95; www.designseptember.be).*

October/November
Brussels Marathon
first weekend in October
Lace up and hit the streets at this annual race that winds through the city's neighborhoods, parks and tree-lined avenues *(Esplanade du Cinquantenaire; 02 11 45 99 99; www.ingbrusselsmarathon.be).*

Flanders International Film Festival
mid-October
This ten-day festival in Ghent, launched in 1974, is Belgium's premier film event. It presents more than 150 full-length and short films to die-hard cinema buffs *(various locations in Ghent; 09 242 80 60; www.filmfestival.be).*

Choco-laté
mid-November
A sweet reason to visit Bruges, this three day festival celebrates the country's favorite confection. A chocolate tasting, chocolate sculpting, kids events, and even chocolate body painting all take place in the medieval Bell Tower *(Bruggemuseum Belfort, Markt 7, Bruges; 11 011 48 07 70; www.choco-late.be).*

Sablon Nights
last weekend in November
Candles and twinkling lights illuminate one of Brussels' most beautiful squares in late November, setting a charming scene worthy of being captured in a snow globe *(Place du Grand Sablon; 02 512 19 00; www.sablon-bruxelles.com).*

December
Winter Wonders
late November–early January
Christmas cheer sprinkles over Brussels from the Grand Place to the Quai au Bois à Bruler, where 240 decorated wooden chalets sell warm wine, holiday cookies and Brussels-themed stocking stuffers. An ice-skating rink, a sledding track,and a Ferris wheel bring even more merriment, while the giant Christmas tree on the Grand Place comes with its own soundtrack and light show *(Quai au Bois à Bruler; www.plaisirsdhiver.be).*

Snow and Ice Sculpture Festival
late November–mid-January
Spectacular ice sculptures carved by professional sculptors and artists adorn the square in front of Bruges' main train station during this popular festival *(Station Square, Bruges; 05 020 04 65; www.icesculpture.be).*

Christmas Market
mid December early January
'Tis the season to head to Antwerp's Grand Square and get into the spirit at the Christmas Market. Enjoy mulled wine, holiday décor, regional sweets and more in a stunning setting *(Grote Markt, Antwerp; www.christmas-markets.org/belgium).*

PRACTICAL INFORMATION

WHEN TO GO

Brussels is worth a visit any time of year, and predicting a good time is easy thanks to its myriad attractions, restaurants, and a jam-packed cultural calendar. Predicting the weather is another story. In a nutshell, the only thing you can count on is that the weather is unpredictable, and that it will dominate the conversation, at least once, on your trip.

sunny days, it seems that half the population of Brussels lingers at outdoor cafés and restaurant terraces, or spreads out on the grass in a park.

Spring

Thanks to all the rain, spring is blooming season in Brussels. A riot of early flowers – tulips, daffodils, hyacinths – enhance the look of Brussels' tree-lined avenues, regal squares and numerous parks. In April, in the Watermael-Boitsfort neighborhood of Brussels, the pink blossoms of cherry trees cheer up residents, while the Bois de Halle in Hallerbos (*15km/9mi south of Brussels*) draws nature lovers to see the forest floor carpeted with tiny bluebells.

Summer

Summer is usually warm, but rarely hot. When it is hot, however, there are few air-conditioned buildings in Brussels (large hotels will have it, of course). On those coveted

Autumn

Autumn is a beautiful time of year and is unpredictable, just like the rest of the seasons. Temperatures begin to cool, and leaves don golden and russet hues. By early November, the leaves lie crisp and brown on the ground, and there is a chill in the air.

Winter

Though winters are generally dark, wet and cold, with blankets of gray draped over the city for long stretches, there is a distinct charm to this season. Experiencing the magical Christmas Market on the Quais au Bois à Bruler, then cozying up to a fire and sipping a cup of hot Belgian chocolate, is not a bad way to spend a day.

Average Seasonal High Temperatures				
	January	**April**	**July**	**October**
Brussels	41°F/5°C	54°F/12°C	72°F/22°C	57°F/14°C
Antwerp	43°F/6°C	57°F/14°C	73°F/23°C	59°F/15°C
Bruges	41°F/5°C	52°F/11°C	72°F/22°C	55°F/13°C
Ghent	43°F/6°C	55°F/13°C	72°F/22°C	59°F/15°C

MUST KNOW

KNOW BEFORE YOU GO
Useful Websites For Planning Your Trip

www.visitbrussels.be – Detailed and up-to-the-minute site run by the communications agency that handles tourism for the Brussels Capital Region.

www.belgique-tourisme.net – Belgian Tourist Office site for visiting Brussels and beyond.

www.visitbelgium.com – Belgian Tourist Office in the Americas site is comprehensive and detailed, with offices and contact information in the US and Canada.

www.bruxellespourtous.be A tourist guidebook for people with reduced mobility.

www.thalys.be – Thalys provides commercial passenger-rail services between Paris, Brussels, Amsterdam and Cologne.

www.brussels-hotels.com – A searchable database by neighborhood and rating.

www.brusselsairport.be – Knowing your way around the airport can save time.

Useful Websites Once You're There

www.sensum.be – A searchable database of Brussels' restaurants, with beautiful photos.

www.musicbrussels.com – Promoting live music from local and international bands.

www.upfront-live.be – From bars to events to good grub, this entertainment site has it all.

www.xpats.com – Geared to expats with local classifieds, news, happenings and more.

www.spottedbylocals.com/ brussels – Locals chime in on where to go, eat and play.

Street sign, Brussels

©JL Ilan Love/Apa Publications

Tourism Offices

Brussels Info Place – The Brussels Info Place, or **BIP**, near the Place Royal, is the visitors center of the Brussels Capital Region and the one place you'll want to stop for maps, brochures and information on cultural and tourist activities. You can even buy tickets for the theater and concerts here *(Rue Royale 2; open daily 9am–6pm; closed Jan 1 & Dec 25; 02 563 63 99; www.biponline.be)*.

More tourist information can be found at:
Brussels National Airport *(Arrivals Hall)*
Gare du Midi *(South Train Station, Central Concourse; Rue de France 40)*
European Parliament *(Rue Wiertz 43)*
Hôtel de Ville *(Grand Place)*

International Visitors
Foreign Embassies in Belgium
(All embassies listed below are in the Upper Town)
American Embassy
Boulevard du Régent 27
+32 02 508 21 11
belgium.usembassy.gov

Australian Embassy
Rue Guimard 6
+32 02 286 05 00
www.belgium.embassy.gov.au

British Embassy
Avenue d'Auderghem 10
+32 02 287 62 11
www.ukinbelgium.fco.gov.uk

Canadian Embassy
Avenue de Tervuren 2
+32 02 741 06 11
www.belgium.gc.ca

Irish Embassy
Chaussée d'Etterbeek 180
+32 02 235 66 76
www.irelandrepbrussels.be

New Zealand Embassy
Square De Meeus 1
+32 02 512 10 40
www.nzembassy.com/belgium

South African Embassy
Rue Montoyer 17-19
+32 02 285 44 00
www.southafrica.be

Belgian Embassy in the US
3330 Garfield St., NW,
Washington, D.C. 20008
202-333-6900;
www.diplobel.us

Entry Requirements
Passports
Citizens of the European Union
entering Belgium need only their
national ID card. A valid passport is
required by anyone else and should
be valid for at least three months
beyond the period of stay. Make
sure you have an adequate number
of unused pages (at least two) in
your passport to allow for stamps
upon arrival and departure.

Bringing Your Pet
If traveling with "Fluffy" or
"Rover," there are special
regulations for pets, and a
general health certificate and
proof of rabies vaccination from
your vet will be needed. Contact
the Belgian embassy or your air
carrier for more information.

Visas
Requirements vary for nationals
of different countries and states;
check before leaving to see which
type of visa you might need for
entry. A visa for entry into Belgium
is not required for citizens of the
EU, US, UK, Canada, New Zealand
or Australia for stays up to 90 days.
A tourist visa is required for South
African nationals.

ID Requirements
Belgian law requires everyone
to carry official identification at
all times. This ID must be shown
upon request by any Belgian police
official. If you are not a resident of
Belgium, you will need to present a
passport or an identity document
issued by another EU member
state, if asked. If you don't have it,
you could be charged a fine.

Customs Regulations
In general, narcotics and other
drugs, explosive material, and
pornographic material are strictly
prohibited from being brought
into Belgium. The importation of
meat, meat products, milk and
milk products is also prohibited.
A special permit is required for
firearms and ammunition of any
kind. Visitors entering Belgium
are limited to bringing in 200
cigarettes (50 cigars or 250 grams

MUST KNOW

of tobacco); 1 liter of spirits over 22% alcohol by volume; and 50 grams of perfume. Other restricted items include medicines and plant material. For more information, check online at *belgium.visahq. com/customs*.

VAT Refunds
Visitors are entitled to a refund of the **Value Added Tax**, or VAT, on certain goods purchased from participating retailers. It's a good idea to ask before you buy, especially if you're considering a big-ticket item. The VAT rate in Belgium is 21%, and there is a €125 minimum charge to apply for the refund. Look for stores with the "Tax Free Shopping" sticker in the window or ask the sales clerk. You will be required to fill out forms and have them stamped at the airport before you leave Belgium. Get more information from Global Blue *(www.global-blue.com)* and Premier Tax Free *(www.premiertaxfree.com)*.

Health
High-quality medical facilities are widely available in Brussels, and large hospitals are equipped to handle almost every medical problem. Staff at hospitals in BrusselsEand in Flemish-speaking

Touring Tip

Unlike in the United States, items such as pain medication, cough syrup or cold remedies must be purchased at a pharmacy in Belgium.

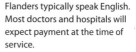

Flanders typically speak English. Most doctors and hospitals will expect payment at the time of service.

Hospitals
Cliniques Universitaires St-Luc
Avenue Hippocrate 10
+32 02 764 11 11
www.saintluc.be

Clinique Edith Cavell
Rue Edith Cavell 32
+32 02 340 40 40
www.chirec.be

Queen Fabiola Children's Hospital
Avenue Jean-Joseph Crocq 15
+32 02 477 33 11
www.huderf.be

Hôpital Erasme
Route de Lennik 808
+32 02 555 31 11
www.erasme.ulb.ac.be

Pharmacies
In Brussels, a *pharmacie* (French) or *apotheek* (Dutch) is clearly marked with a bright green, usually flashing, cross. Most are open during the week from 9am to 6pm, as well as on Saturday mornings. In each neighborhood, there is usually one pharmacy that is open late at night *(for information, call 09 001 05 00 or check online at www.pharmacie.be)*.

Find a Doctor
While many doctors around Brussels work in clinics and hospitals, many also work from offices set up in their homes. The website **www.mgbru.be** allows you to search for family doctors by area of Brussels and language spoken. The American Embassy also has a list of English-speaking doctors and dentists.

Language

Belgium has three official languages: French, Dutch and German. French is spoken in the south (Wallonia); Dutch in the north (Flanders); and in certain eastern provinces, you'll hear German. **Brussels** has two official languages: French and Flemish. While streets, menus, products and signs are labeled in both languages, there is no question that French is the *lingua franca* of Brussels. Thanks to the dozens of international organizations here, English is widely understood and spoken too.

Language Schools

Given the influx of foreigners into Brussels and the proclivity of Belgians toward mastering multiple foreign tongues, language schools are numerous here. Offering a pleasant *"goedemorgen,"* a sincere *"merci,"* or asking for exactly what you need enhances the travel experience no matter where you go, so why not say *oui* or *ja* to a few classes?

Berlitz

Avenue Louise 306–310
+32 02 649 61 75
www.berlitz.be
Avenue de Tervuren 265
+32 02 763 14 14
www.berlitz.be

Amira

Rue du Trône 14–16
+32 02 640 68 50
www.amira.be

Alliance Francaise

Rue de la Loi 26
+32 02 788 21 60
www.alliancefr.be

GETTING THERE
By Air

The main international airport for Belgium, **Brussels National Airport** *(airport helpdesk: 09 007 00 00; www.brusselsairport.be)* is located 14km/8mi northeast of the city center. Most major international airlines fly to and from this airport, also called Zaventem, the name of the town in which it resides. Easy Jet, Brussels Airlines and other regional carriers, also fly from Zaventem.

Airport Transportation

A **taxi** to the city center will run you approximately €45, and there is a good **rail** connection from the airport *(lower level)* to the North, South, and Central train stations in Brussels *(trains depart every 20min between 5:30am–12:20am from the airport and 4:45am–11:10pm from the city; €5,20; www.b-rail.com).* If you're taking the train into the city from the airport, buy your ticket before boarding to avoid a surcharge.

There's also a **bus** link *(no. 12; 30min)* between the airport and Place Schuman in the European Quarter *(Mon–Fri 6am–8pm; €3; 02 1631 37 37;*

Brussels' Other Airport

The city has another airport called **Brussels-South Charleroi** *(www.charleroi-airport.com),* which is located about 55km/ 34mi south of Brussels, in the city of Charleroi.
Several low-cost air carriers like **Ryan Air** and **Wizzair** fly from here. You can get to the airport by train or bus from the Gare du Midi station in Brussels; the ride takes about an hour.

www.stib.be). On weekends, and after 8pm Mon–Fri, take bus no. 21.

Airlines

Most major airlines fly in and out of Brussels National Airport. Customer-service desks are located in the main departures hall (some are open only in the morning, so call ahead).

Aer Lingus
+32 07 035 99 01
www.aerlingus.com

American Airlines
+32 07 027 27 00
www.americanairlines.be

British Airways
+32 02 717 32 17
www.britishairways.com

Brussels Airlines
+32 02 723 23 45
www.brusselsairlines.com

Continental Airlines
+32 02 643 39 39
www.continental.com

Delta Airlines
+32 07 030 08 72
www.delta.com

Take Your Car
If you're travelling from the UK, why not bring your car? The trip between Folkestone, England, and Calais, France, through the Channel Tunnel takes just 35 minutes. Then it's a 200km/124mi-drive to Brussels. The number of departures depends on the volume of traffic *(trains depart three to four times per hour during the day and one to two times per hour from midnight to 6am; 08 705 353 535; www.eurotunnel.com).*

United Airlines
+32 02 713 36 00
www.unitedairlines.be

By Train
Thalys high-speed trains *(www.thalys.com)* link Brussels with cities in Germany, the Netherlands and France, including Amsterdam and Paris.
Arriving in Brussels via **Eurostar** (www.eurostar.com) from the United Kingdom is a fun experience. Frequent trains travel via the Channel Tunnel between St. Pancras International Station in

Thalys high-speed train

©Thalys International

London and the Gare du Midi (south station) in Brussels. The travel time is two hours.

By Boat

Cross-channel service from the United Kingdom to mainland Europe, for individuals and cars, can be booked with these companies:

Norfolkline
0870 870 10 20
www.norfolkline-ferries.com
(Dover–Dunkirk)

P&O Ferries
0871 664 56 45
www.poferries.com
(Dover–Calais)

Sea France
0871 663 25 46
www.seafrance.com
(Dover–Calais)

Viamare
0208 206 34 20
www.viamare.com
(Dover–Calais)

GETTING AROUND
By Train

Brussels' three main train stations are: **Gare du Midi** *(south; Rue de France 40)*, **Gare Centrale** *(central; Rue des Colonies 10)*, and **Gare du Nord** *(north; Rue de Progrès 6)*.

Eurail Pass
Non-European residents can travel within Europe using a discounted Eurail Pass. A one-country pass starts at $51; a Regional Pass (two countries) starts at $187; and a Select Pass (three, four or five countries) starts at $329 *(www.eurail.com)*.

Eurostar and Thalys trains arrive and depart from Gare du Midi. There are metro and bus connections at all three stations.

By Bus

The **Société des Transports Intercommunaux de Bruxelles** *(STIB; wwwstib.be)* is the largest Belgian urban public-transport company, and serves the 19 communes of Brussels as well as 11 other outlying communities. The STIB network includes 4 metro lines, 19 tram lines, 50 bus lines and 11 night-bus lines. Tickets can be purchased at any metro station, as well as at newsstands, supermarkets, and numerous other locations. *For tickets and fares, see Public Transportation (p28).*

By Taxi

You can't hail a cab on a street in Brussels because drivers are forbidden to pick up customers within 100m/328ft of a taxi stand. Call a licensed taxi service for pickup, or if you are at a hotel or restaurant, ask them to call a cab for you. The meter starts at €2.40 *(€4.40 after 10pm)* and calculates at €1.23/km within Brussels' 19 communes. This fare doubles if you're traveling outside the city.

A couple of omnipresent taxi companies in Brussels are:
Taxi Verts – (Green Taxis) 02 349 49 49; www.taxisverts.be.
Taxis Bleus – (Blue Taxis) 02 268 00 00; www.taxisbleus.be.

By Car

Feeling brave and don't mind congested roads and a complex underground tunnel network? Are you curious about the confusing

Car Rental		
Car Rental Company	🖉**Reservations**	**Website**
Alamo	02 715 87 30	www.alamo.com
Avis	07 022 30 01	www.avis.com
Budget	02 721 50 97	www.budget.com
Europcar	02 348 92 12	www.europcar.com
Hertz	02 717 32 01	www.hertz.com
Sixt	02 753 25 60	www.sixt.com

priorité à droite rule that gives any vehicle on your right the priority, even on major roads? If you answered "yes," then driving in Brussels is the sport for you! Keep in mind that, as in any large city, parking is scarce and garages and hotels charge a premium daily rate.

Rental Cars
A number of rental-car agencies are located in the airport arrivals hall (go to your right when you exit baggage claim). To rent a car, you must have a valid driver's license, a photo ID or passport and a credit card in your name.

Rules of the Road
The maximum speed limit on motorways in Belgium is 120kph/74mph. Speed limits within built-up areas are 50kph/31mph unless otherwise posted (30kph/18mph in school areas). Speeding is heavily fined.

Gas (petrol) is sold by the liter in Belgium (1 liter = 0.26 gallons). Distances are posted in kilometers (1km = 0.6mi). The legal minimum age for driving is 18 years. All drivers must carry a valid license, certificate of insurance, vehicle registration or rental contract, and passport or proof of identity.

These two organizations in Brussels provide assistance in case of a breakdown:

The Royal Automobile Club of Belgium *(Rue d'Arlon 53, 1040, Brussels; 07 815 20 00; www.racb.com).*

Touring Club of Belgium *(Rue de la Loi 44, 1040 Brussels; 07 034 47 77; www.touring.be).*

When driving in Belgium, keep the following rules in mind:

* Drive on the right side of the road.
* At an intersection, the driver on the right always has priority, unless otherwise indicated.
* Seat belts are compulsory for all passengers.
* Children up to 36kg/79lbs must ride in an approved child-safety seat (offered by most rental-car agencies; request these when you reserve your rental car).
* Trams have the right of way over other vehicles.
* While driving, cellular telephones may be used only with a hands-free system.
* Do not drink and drive.

Traffic Signs in Belgium		
English	**French**	**Flemish**
Exit	Sortie	Uitrit
Entrance	Entrée	Toegang
Detour	Déviation	Wegomlegging
Highway	Autoroute	Verkeersweg
No entry	Sens interdit	Verboden toegang
One-way street	Sens unique	Eenrichtingsverkeer
Bus lane	Couloir pour autobus	Busstrook
Speed restriction	Ralentissement	Snelheidsvermindering
Traffic circle	Rondpoint	Verkeersplein

In Case of Accident

Drivers involved in an accident must stop and help injured people, collaborate in avoiding danger and other possible accidents, and call the police *(dial 101)* if there are injured people or if the road cannot be cleared.

By Public Transportation

Brussels has a cheap and integrated network of public transportation incorporating trams, underground trains (metro) and buses, with tickets usable on any of the three means of transport.

This public transport network, run by the **Société des Transports Intercommunaux de Bruxelles** or **STIB** *(www.stib.be)*, operates from 5am to midnight, depending on the location. Maps and schedules are available at any train or metro station, and are posted at each bus stop.

Tickets, called **Jumps**, are sold at metro stations, SNBC stations, online, or onboard buses and trams in single- *(€1,80)*, five- *(€7,30)* or ten-trip *(€11.20)* increments, as well as one-, three-, and five-day passes. Individual tickets *(€2)* can be purchased from drivers aboard trams and buses. A ticket must

be validated by sliding it through the orange machines located in metro stations and onboard trams and buses. Tickets are valid for one hour, and you can transfer as many times as you wish to within that time.

Brussels Metro

The city's subway system consists of a network of 59 stations served by four lines (1, 2, 5, 6) with some shared sections. The pre-metro network in Brussels has two underground sections (lines 3 and 4) used by trams and designed to be convertible to conventional metro lines. Metro stations are marked with a white letter **M** on a blue background.

The Brussels Card

This tourist card offers unlimited rides on public transportation as well as free access to 32 museums, and other discounts around Brussels, for one, two or three days, *(€24, €34, or €40 respectively).* Buy it online at *www.brusselscard.be* or purchase one at the **Brussels Info Place** (BIP) on Place Royale.

Line 1 runs from Gare de l'Ouest (West Station) through western Brussels to Stockel/Stokkel at the east end.
Line 2 is a loop starting and ending in Simonis (Elizabeth) via the eastern side of the Little Ring Road.

PRACTICAL INFORMATION

29

Line 3 runs from the Churchill stop south of Brussels to the Esplanade stop on the north end.

Line 4 runs from the Gare du Nord (North Station) to the Stalle parking lot at the south end of the city.

Line 5 runs from Erasme to the south, then west of Brussels to Herrmann, and from Debroux to the southeast.

Line 6 runs from Roi Baudouin to the north, then west of Brussels to Simonis (Léopold II).

The **De Lijn line** runs suburban buses to locations around Flanders *(www.delijn.be)*.

By Bicycle

Like driving, biking on the main roads of Brussels is not for the faint of heart. However, drivers are used to bikes, and roads through the parks and smaller neighborhoods can be pleasant routes by which to explore the capital. Bike lanes are clearly marked on the main roads, separated from traffic.

ACCESSIBILITY

New buildings in Brussels are required by law to be accessible to people with reduced mobility, and most of the large hotels easily accommodate wheelchairs. Many older buildings are not equipped to handle disabled visitors; call ahead to check. Bear in mind that squares like the Grand Place and other historic streets have uneven cobbled pavement and might not be easy to navigate with a wheelchair. Smaller restaurants and cafés are not likely to have handicapped-accessible toilets.

MOBIB

A new chip card system called MOBIB is slowly being introduced in Brussels and will replace the Jump paper-ticket system. Journeys with a MOBIB card are slightly cheaper *(€1,60 for a single trip)*. However for tourists, it's an inconvenient and cumbersome process. As it stands now, you have to pay a €5 deposit for a MOBIB card and you must provide a photo ID. The jury is out on how this will work for visitors.

Public transport is becoming more accommodating to people with reduced mobility. Metro stations have been equipped with Braille information panels and floor-level tactile guides. But some stations still have escalator- and stair-only access to get in and out.

STIB has a minibus equipped to transport a disabled traveler from door to door. Book in advance at 02 515 23 65 or www.stib.be.

Useful Websites for Travelers with Disabilities

www.toevla.be –
Find information about accessibility at buildings and tourist sites.

www.travelintelligence.com –
Online travel sight with searchable information about accessibility.

BASIC INFORMATION
Accommodations
See Must Stay for details and a list of suggested places to stay.

Business Hours

Banks

Banks are usually open Monday – Friday 9am–4pm and are closed on Saturdays, Sundays and holidays. Some banks will close for an hour during lunch.

Museums

Most museums are open from Tuesday through Sunday (though smaller museums may close on Sunday). Generally, museums are closed on Monday.

Shops

Shops are normally open 9am–6pm from Monday through Saturday. In the Marolles neighborhood of Brussels, many shops are open on Sunday and closed on Monday. Almost all bakeries, butchers, cheese shops, fishmongers, etc., close on Mondays. Some smaller family-run businesses also close Wednesday afternoon, when children are out of school. **Pharmacies** generally close for lunch, between noon and 2pm. It's best to call ahead or check hours online before you go.

Money

Since 2002, the **euro** has been the currency of Belgium, and the

Euros

©Maria Toutoudaki/iStockphoto

former Belgian Franc has been phased out of circulation. Euro banknotes come in denominations of €5, €10, €20, €50, €100, €200 and €500. You will also find coins in demominations of €1 and €2; these come in handy for metro tickets and tipping.

ATMs

For some mysterious reason, ATMs are not as ubiquitous in the center of Brussels as they are in other major capitals. If you find one, mark your map! There is one at the bottom of the Eurostar escalators in the Gare du Midi train station, and a couple in the arrivals hall of the airport. There are ATMs inside

Important Phone Numbers	
Emergencies	☏ **112**
Fire Department or ambulance	☏ 100
Police	☏ 101
Belgian Red Cross (24-hour ambulance service)	☏ 105
Directory assistance in English	☏ 1414
Directory assistance in Flemish	☏ 1212
Directory assistance in French	☏ 1313

banks, but you may need that bank's specific ATM card to get through the security door to access them.

Credit Cards

Most hotels, shops and restaurants accept Visa and MasterCard. American Express cards are generally accepted at larger hotels and shops, but not at smaller restaurants and boutiques.
To report a stolen credit card:
American Express – 02 676 21 21; www.americanexpress.com.
Master Card – 08 001 50 96 (*toll free*); www.mastercard.com/be.
Visa – 070 344 344; www.visaeurope.com.

Currency Exchange

The best and cheapest way to obtain the local currency is by using an ATM, but given the difficulty of finding one in Brussels, you might have to use a bank teller or an exchange bureau. The latter can be found in the arrivals hall at the airport, at the Gare du Midi and Gare Centrale train stations, and around the Grand Place. A fee is charged for the transaction.

Electricity

In Belgium, the voltage runs at 220 volts A/C. Plugs are two round pins; adaptors are available from airports and many electrical shops. Hotels usually have extras too.

Internet

The Internet is widely available in hotels and some cafés and restaurants. The **fnac** department store on Rue Neuve (*in City 2 mall*) has a cyber café; and **Café de la Presse** (*Avenue Louise 493; see Must Eat*), in Ixelles, gives you a code if you want to have a cup of coffee or a snack while you surf.

Smoking

Smoking is forbidden in most public spaces (metro, trams, buses, railway stations, airports, churches). In most cafés and restaurants there are separate sections for smokers. Smoking is allowed on outdoor restaurant terraces.

Telephones

Pay phones are fast becoming relics of the telecommunications past, but occasionally you need one. A few do exist around Brussels, but they are hard to spot (good bets are train stations and main shopping areas). Pay phones take a prepaid phone card, available at newsstands, post offices, supermarkets and train stations. Most people travel with cell phones these days, and there are three main mobile-phone networks in Belgium, all of them offering monthly subscription or pay-as-you-go cards. Branches of these stores are found all over Brussels:

MUST KNOW

English Language Bookstores

If you don't read French or Flemish, you can find books in English at the following shops.

Cook & Book – *Avenue Paul Hymans 251. 02 761 26 00. www.cookandbook.be.* This bookstore universe, a destination in itself, comprises nine connected shops, with a few restaurants in between. Books are organized by specialty, including English-language titles.

Sterling Books – *Fossé aux Loups 38. 02 223 62 23. www.sterlingbook.be.* The largest independent English-language bookstore in Brussels offers more than 40,000 titles.

Waterstone's – *Boulevard Adolphe Max 71. 02 219 27 08. www.waterstones.com.* This enormous bookshop, part of a British chain, boasts a staff of bilingual book lovers. Expect a wide range of subjects and a large selection of magazines and newspapers in English.

Proximus – Boulevard du Roi Albert II 27; www.proximus.be.
Mobistar – Avenue de la Toison d'Or 18; www.mobistar.be.
Base – Rue Neerveld 105; www.base.be.

Calls Within Brussels
Within Brussels, you don't need to dial 32, but you do need to dial a zero before the phone number. To complicate matters, if you are calling a mobile phone in Brussels (numbers that start with 04), you don't need the 02. Simply dial 04 and the 7-digit number.
From the **US to Brussels** – dial 011+32 +2 (no zero) + the 7-digit number. From **Brussels to the US** – dial 00 +1+ area code + 7-digit number. From the **UK to Brussels** – dial 00 32 + 2 (no zero) + the 7-digit number.

Tipping
Tipping is not necessary at restaurants, though most people throw in a few coins if the service is good. Taxi fares include the tip, but drivers still expect a little extra, as do attendants at the cinema and theater restrooms.

Time Zone
Belgium is one hour ahead of Greenwich Mean Time, and six hours ahead of Eastern Standard Time in the US.

Cook & Book

© By2 Photographers

PRACTICAL INFORMATION

CAPITAL OF EUROPE

In the not-so-distant past, Brussels was often just a pass-through point for travelers and backpackers enroute to more glamorous neighbors Paris and Amsterdam. Those who did get off the train snapped the essential photos of the **Grand Place★★★** and the **Mannekin Pis★★**, sipped some beer, then checked Brussels off the "been there, done that" list. Happily, times have changed, and travelers who give Brussels more than just a passing glance are learning what residents have known all along – that Brussels is a city that unravels its secrets slowly, and it is anything but boring.

Boasting more than 2,000 restaurants, a burgeoning cultural scene, world-class museums, and hundreds of acres of forests and parks that have earned the city the title of "Greenest Capital in Europe," Brussels is a vibrant place. Thanks to the headquarters of NATO, the European Union, several highly ranked universities, and the myriad multinational corporations that all call Brussels home, the streets pulse with an international esprit. (An estimated 27 percent of the city's 1 million inhabitants hail from outside Belgium.)

Spend time in the square called **Place du Luxembourg**, wander the streets of the African **Matongé** neighborhood, or shop at the **Midi Market**, and you'll hear dialects and accents from many continents. No wonder Brussels is called "The Capital of Europe."

The Medieval City
Brussels emerged at the end of the 10C when Charles, Duke of Lower Lotharingia, had a castle built on **Île St-Géry**, an island formed by two branches of the little Senne River. The settlement was named Bruocsella, a Frankish word meaning "the village in the marshes." Brussels quickly developed as a trading city on the highway between Flanders and Cologne, and the **St. Michael's Church** (now the Cathedral of Saints Michael and Gudula), was built on Treurenberg Hill as a sign of the town's prosperity. In 1047,

Royal Palace

©Mediasky/visitbrussels.be

St. Michael's became a collegiate church, dedicated to the virgin St. Gudula.

The early town was defended by a wall of ramparts, built in the 12C and 14C. The wall's line followed what is now the Little Ring Road, called the *Petite Ceinture* (French for "little belt"), that circles the modern city's core. In the 15C Brussels turned to the arts, influenced by the dukes of Burgundy. A magnificent city hall (the Hôtel de Ville) was built, and the streets were adorned with fountains. Trades here in the 1500s specialized in fabrics such as **tapestries** and **lace** – works of art in themselves – that were sold in lucrative markets in Europe.

Capital of the Low Countries

In 1516, **Emperor Charles V** was crowned in St. Gudula's Church. The governor, Mary of Hungary, settled in Brussels in 1531, and the city replaced Mechelen as the seat of government of the Low Countries. Charles V abdicated his title at the Palace of Coudenberg in October 1555, handing over sovereignty of the Low Countries to his son **Philip II**. Philip drew Brussels into the religious strife of the 16C, leading to an armed uprising against Spanish rule. In 1575, the city, which had by then shaken off Spanish rule, was recaptured. The city suffered again in 1695 when the French besieged Brussels, hoping to end the siege of the nearby enclave of Namur. For much of the 18C, Brussels was the seat of Austrian rule over the Low Countries. Governor Charles of Lorraine established a glittering court life here and did much to embellish the city. Austrian rule foundered at the end of the century; in 1795 the southern Netherlands became part of Republican France, and Brussels was demoted from capital city to a mere "country town." After Napoleon's defeat at nearby Waterloo in 1815, the city once more became the capital of the reunited Netherlands.

Capital of Belgium

Union with Holland proved unpopular. The "September Days" uprising of 1830 led to the Belgian provinces separating from Holland and becoming an independent kingdom, with Brussels as its capital. **King Léopold I** made his ceremonial entry into the city on July 21, 1831. That same year, the **National Congress** established

It's Reigning Men

Following Belgium's independence from the Netherlands, its monarchs have all been men:

Léopold I	1831–1865
Léopold II	1865–1909
Albert I	1909–1934
Léopold III	1934–1951
Baudouin I	1951–1993
Albert II	1993–present

Belgium's first constitution. In 1835, continental Europe's first passenger railway began operating from Brussels to Mechelen.

The Builder King

Though disliked by his subjects at the end of his reign, due to his ravaging of the African Congo, **King Léopold II** is remembered today as the "Builder King." He launched several major architectural projects during his reign that give Brussels its modern profile. The **Triumphal**

Mannekin Pis, see p59

©The Print Collector/age fotostock

Arch at **Cinquantenaire Park**, the **Royal Greenhouses★★** and the surrounding park in Laeken, as well as the **Japanese Tower** and the **Chinese Pavilion**, were all realized by Léopold II. The King was also responsible for founding the **Royal Museum for Central Africa★★★** in nearby Tervuren.

A New Post-War City

Belgium was one of the first signatories of the UN charter in June 1945, joined the Organization for European Economic Co-operation in 1948, and became the Headquarters of the European Economic Community (EEC) in 1957. Brussels' new role at the forefront of the new Europe, combined with the pressing need for post-war reconstruction, saw many of the city's buildings razed by developers. In the 1960s, despite strong resistance, buildings like the Maison du Peuple (designed by Victor Horta) were destroyed. Some of the poorer districts were totally bulldozed. The demolished buildings were replaced by tall, bland, multistory structures. When the Gare du Midi was linked by a tunnel to the Gare du Nord, it transformed the district between the Upper and Lower towns. The **Mont des Arts** quarter also took on a whole new appearance.

Expo '58, the 1958 World's Fair, saw the building of the **Atomium★** as well as tunnels under the city's Little Ring Road. Brussels became the headquarters of NATO in 1967, the same year that the behemoth glass and steel Berlaymont Building became the main office of the European Economic Community.

Royal Greenhouses

©Olivier Polet/visitbrussels.be

Brussels Divided

Surrounded by the Flemish province of Vlaams-Brabant, Brussels became the site of a notorious language divide in 1962 when French-speaking Wallonia and Flemish-speaking-Flanders declared themselves separate entities, giving the city an official bilingual status. In 1965, the political parties also split into French and Flemish camps. Successive Belgian governments granted more and more auto-nomy to these communities and changed Belgium from a centralized to a federal state. Also during this time, **King Baudouin I** earned the love and respect of the Belgian people for granting independence to the Belgian Congo and for keeping Belgium from separating into Flemish and French states. Since Baudouin had no children of his own, upon his death, the crown passed to his brother, **King Albert II**.

In 2001, the Treaty of Nice reformed the institutional structure of the European Union to allow for eastward expansion, and declaring Brussels as the capital of Europe. As Europe quickly expanded, a new influx of diplomats and European Union employees from member countries landed in Brussels.

Growing Pains

Today, the most critical battle facing Brussels is tackling the heated political and linguistic debates, including the threat of separation, that still menace the country. Belgium is split in two horizontally and also linguistically, with Brussels geographically stuck in the middle. A rift between Belgium's Flemish-speaking and French-speaking camps brought negotiations over forming a government to a standstill on June 13, 2010; since then (and as of press time), there is no federal government in Belgium. Despite its political problems, Brussels reveals its beauty to visitors in the patchwork of eclectic neighborhoods that knit together to form one of the most dynamic cities in Europe – and a place of endless surprises for those willing to get off the train and stay a while.

NEIGHBORHOODS

Most people arriving in Brussels concentrate on the center, but to really see the city, it's essential to understand its patchwork of neighborhoods. Each has its own unique personality that combines to create this diverse and vibrant international city. Much like Paris is divided into areas called *arrondissements*, Brussels carves itself into 19 municipalities known as communes, each locally governed. While the best way to explore the city center is on foot, Brussels' well-connected network of subway and tram lines can transport you to the outer communes with ease.

LOWER TOWN

The area below the escarpment dividing the city is where modern Brussels was born. Occupied by Celtic and Germanic tribes (The Belgae), the area that is now Brussels was bleak and savage, marked by a topography of marshy land and floodplains formed by the uncontainable Senne River.

It wasn't until the year 1000 that a church, dedicated to St. Géry, was built on Ile St-Géry in the river; this would become the genesis of the city of Brussels. St-Géry still exists, and nowadays **Place St-Géry**

Comic Strip Art

Brussels reigns as the comic-strip capital of the world. Such international icons as Tintin, the Smurfs, Spirou, Lucky Luke and Astérix all got their start in this city. A temple to the "funnies," the **Belgian Center for Comic Strip Art★★** *(see Museums)* occupies a beautifully renovated Art Nouveau building.

Grab a map, available at the museum or at the tourist office in the Hôtel de Ville on Grand Place, and follow the **Comic Strip Trail** of murals painted on buildings and walls around the city *(see Ideas and Tours).*

(see Historic Squares) is the hub of the city's nightlife. From the square, you can walk along the Rue de Borgval, one of the original village streets.

Lower Town still beats as the heart of modern Brussels, but pieces of its past are everywhere you look. From the labyrinthine pattern of streets to the last vestiges of the settlement's defensive wall – the **Anneessens Tower** *(see Grand Architecture)* and the Black Tower (Tour Noire), behind St. Catherine's Church – Brussels history reveals itself at every turn. Encompassing the **Grand Place★★★** as well as some of the city's other iconic sites, the Lower Town is the first stop for visitors.

Top Three Things To Do in Lower Town

+ **Stand awestruck in the Grand Place★★★**
  You have to see Brussels' breathtaking main square to fully appreciate its grandeur *(see Historic Squares).*
+ **Sample chocolate on the Place du Grand Sablon★**
  Several of Belgium's best chocolatiers have set up shop in this striking square *(see Historic Squares).*

- **Tickle your funny bone**
  From Tintin to the Smurfs, Brussels loves its comic-strip characters. Come meet them at the **Belgian Center for Comic Strip Art★★** *(see Museums)*.

Grand Place★★★

Anyone you ask will tell you to start your visit to Brussels at the awe-inspiring main square. As far back as the mid-19C, French writer Victor Hugo couldn't resist its charms, calling it "the most beautiful square in the world." Construction of Grand Place began in the 15C with the market halls and trade-guild houses. In 1695, the French bombarded the square for three days, razing everything except the **Hôtel de Ville** (City Hall; *see Grand Architecture*), which takes up the entire southwest side of the square. Remarkably, the square was rebuilt in less than five years. You can – and should – spend hours here, taking the city's pulse and appreciating the ornate **guildhalls★★★** *(see Grand Architecture)* – each with its wn fascinating story to tell.

Touring Tip

The line between Lower Town and Upper Town is often fuzzy, but geographically the two sections are divided by an escarpment that runs north to south from the end of Rue Royale to the **Palace of Justice**. For ease of navigation, in this guide we use the stretch of Rue de la Regence that runs from the Palace of Justice across **Place Royale★**, where it turns into Rue Royale and continues to **Le Botanique** cultural center, as an unofficial but easy-to-follow frontier.

Place du Grand Sablon★

This elegant square takes its name from the sandy marshes (*sablon* is French for "sand") that once covered the hills dominating the Senne River Valley. In 1299, the hill located south of the city ramparts was used as a cemetery for St. Jean Hospital. Five years later, the hospital gave part of its land to the Guild of Crossbowmen to build a

Grand Place

©Luc Viatour GFDL/visitbrussels.be

NEIGHBORHOODS

39

Today, this square is lined with gabled homes and some of Brussels' most popular restaurants, **Lola** *(no. 33; see Must Eat)* and **Au Vieux Saint-Martin** *(no. 38)*. An **antiques market** occurs every weekend next to the church, no doubt inspired by the numerous antiques shops hidden on streets around the square. A more recent phenomenon is the appearance of chocolate boutiques, like the flagship store of young Belgian chocolatier **Pierre Marcolini** *(Rue des Minimes 1)*, and **Wittamer**, both a shop and a café *(Place du Grand Sablon 13)*.

chapel. **Our Lady of Sablon★** *(see Churches)* still dominates the top of the square. Until 1754, a horse market took place here every Friday, thanks to an artificial water reservoir that served both as a drinking trough for the animals and as water reserves for the city in case of fire. The reservoir was replaced by a fountain in 1661, which was replaced again in 1751 by the more ornate fountain seen today at the bottom of the square.

Rue des Bouchers★

Just off the Grand Place, the narrow pedestrian streets Rue des Bouchers and Petite Rue des Bouchers are often called "Brussels' Belly" due to the plethora of international restaurants that line them.

Les Marolles

Anchored by the **Church of Our Lady of the Chapel** and the **Palace of Justice**, the Marolles neighborhood of Brussels was once home to laborers who produced luxury goods in factories along the river. Les Marolles slowly deteriorated after the bricking over of the Senne forced industry out of the city. Today, this blue-collar quarter is undergoing a bit of a renaissance. Smoky bars and clubs mingle with trendy restaurants such as **L'Idiot du Village** *(Rue Notre-Seigneur 19; see Must Eat)*, and the façades of smart home-décor boutiques rub elbows

Rue des Bouchers

©Heinz-Dieter Falkenst/age fotostock

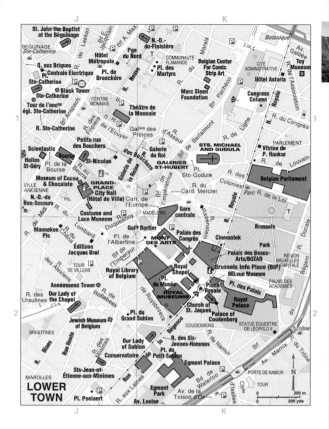

with shabby-chic antiques shops along the parallel Rue Haute and Rue Blaes. A Brussels tradition, the 100-year-old flea market, the **Vieux Marché**, is held daily on the **Place du Jeu de Balle** *(see Shopping)*.

UPPER TOWN

Upper Town is dominated by Coudenberg Hill, where a palace of the same name once presided over the area. From here, both royalty and the bourgeoisie were able to look down upon the less fortunate subjects crammed into the Lower Town. The elevated location also provided a defensive position, allowing for easy spotting of enemies, and keeping royalty a safe distance from the constantly flooding and disease-infested Senne River.

Today, the quarter, home to the ruling government and the royal family, retains a sense of superiority over the Lower Town. Besides the **Royal Palace** *(see Châteaux and Palaces)*, many of the city's best museums – including the **Museum of Ancient Art**★★★, the **Museum of Musical Instruments**★★★, the

41

The Painter's House

Les Marolles' most famous resident was the 16C painter **Pieter Bruegel the Elder** *(see sidebar, p77)*. Though it's not open to the public, Breugel's former home, at Rue Haute 132, is marked by a small plaque.

Cinquantenaire Museum★★★ and the **Magritte Museum★★** *(see Museums for all four)* are located in the Upper Town.

Top Three Things To Do in Upper Town

♦ **Discover fine art**
Whether it's the Old Masters of the 15C, ancient Greek antiquities or more modern works you fancy, Upper Town's cultural museums are sure to satisfy your hunger for the arts.

♦ **Live like royalty**
. . . Or just pretend you do. Each year, for a limited time, the **Royal Palace** opens its doors free of charge to the public, and you can tour the stately rooms where His Majesty the King holds court.

♦ **Wander Cinquantenaire Park**
The **Triumphal Arch** forms the entrance to this manicured park, which is laced with pathways and statues.

Place Royale★

This square atop Coudenberg Hill, which separates Rue de La Régence from Rue Royale and looks down on the slopes of the **Mont Des Arts** area, was once the market square for **Coudenberg Palace**. When the palace burned down in 1731, the area was abandoned for nearly 40 years. In the 1770s, efforts were made to redevelop the entire "Court District." Ruins of the old palace and surrounding buildings were demolished, and a new square, the Place Royale, was edged with the Neoclassical buildings.

European Quarter
(Quartier Européan)

The cobbled streets and grand architecture of the Royal Quarter give way to the institutionalized European Quarter *(see Ideas and Tours)* at the top of Rue de la Loi. In the 1960s, much of the 19C architecture here was demolished to make room for offices. The streets around serene **Leopold Park** *(see Parks and Gardens)* suffered a similar blow when the

Place du Luxembourg

©Marcel Vanhulst/visitbrussels.be

European Quarter

©Marcel Vanhulst/visitbrussels.be

leviathan Espace Léopold complex, which includes the European Parliament, was erected in 2008. **Cinquantenaire Park** *(see Parks and Gardens)* marks the end of the European Quarter and borders the commune of Etterbeek. Here you'll find the **Maison Antoine** *(see Must Eat)*, a popular place for *frites* (French fries) on Place Jourdan.

Place du Luxembourg

Stand in this Neoclassical square and you'll immediately notice the small building with the clock and rounded pediment, which looks like the diminutive twin to the European Parliament looming behind it. This was once the main hall of the train station Gare du Luxembourg.

The station is still here, though it's underground, and the building is now an information center. These days, the terraces of the restaurants and bars around Place Lux, as it's known to locals, fill up after work with business people from the surrounding European institutions. The cacophony of the many accents in their animated conversations harmonizes into a distinct international soundtrack.

Place Ambiorix and Place Marie-Louise

As the Brussels suburbs expanded at the end of the 19C, architect Gédéon Bordiau arranged a series of squares along a slope of land that followed what was once the course of the Maelbeek stream. Today these two adjoining squares show off a cascade of gardens and water features, as well as sculptures by the likes of **Constantin Meunier**.

Place Ambiorix lays claim to several Art Nouveau houses, including the spectacular **Maison St-Cyr** *(no. 11)*. Only 3.5m/11.5ft wide, the house was built for painter Léonard St-Cyr by Gustave Stauven, an apprentice of architect Victor Horta.

Charlotte Was Here

Writer **Charlotte Brontë** (1816–1855) taught in Brussels from 1842 to 1844. She lived on Rue d'Isabelle, near the Place Royale. Brontë fans can see the Rue d'Isabelle underneath the **BELvue Museum★** *(see Museums)*.

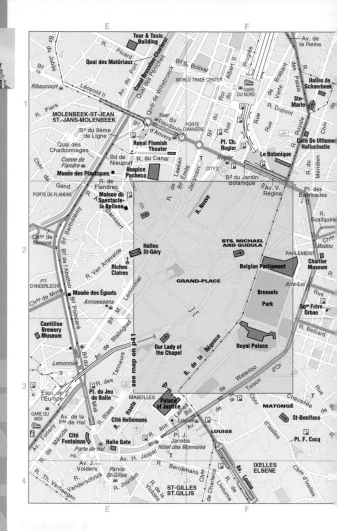

see map on p41

European Union in Brussels

Capital of one of the six founding countries of the EU (the others are France, Germany, Luxembourg, Italy and the Netherlands), Brussels has been the seat of European institutions since 1997. The European Commission, Council and Parliament are all located in the European Quarter, an area bounded by Brussels Park, Cinquantenaire Park and Leopold Park. The EU institutions take up a quarter of the city's available office space, and contribute significantly to Brussels' economy.

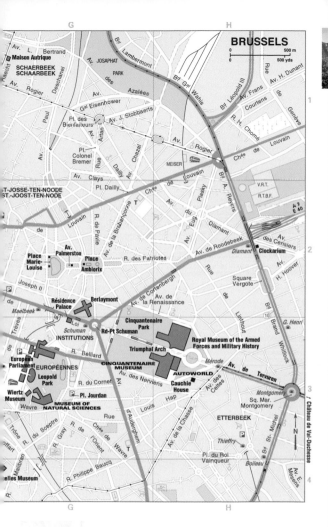

Antique Maps

While in Brussels, have a look in the shops for antique maps of Belgium. These two-dimensional plans provide an interesting overview of the geographical and political ebbs and flows of the country, where conquering rulers and revolutions have changed the borders and the kingdom's name over the past centuries. It's a great way to get an overall perspective of the city and the country, and to see how the region's geography dictated its destiny.

NORTH OF CENTER

Head north of the Little Ring Road that surrounds the historic center of Brussels and you'll discover an odd patchwork of communes, completely dissimilar, yet each having something to offer the visitor. **Laeken** is by far the most visited. Stretching over a huge green area, the town is home to the **Royal Castle** *(see Chateaux and Palaces)* and its surrounding park, which enfolds the **Royal Greenhouses★★** *(see Grand Architecture)*. The quirky **Atomium★** and the **Mini Europe** theme park *(see Family Fun for both)* are also big draws.

Once a wooded hunting ground for city folks, **Schaerbeek** was later known for its cherry orchards. These days Schaerbeek is no longer so bucolic, marred by the Gare du Nord train station and the adjacent red-light district.

Along the Chaussée de Haecht toward St-Josse, you'll find some Moroccan shops, as well as the **Maison Autrique** *(Chaussée de Haecht 266)*, the first house Victor Horta designed.

The smallest commune, **St-Josse** nestles up against the city center. Though it has a host of family-run North African and Turkish eateries, the commune's biggest attractions are its shopping street, **Chaussée de Louvain**, and **Le Botanique** *(see Performing Arts)*, just a hop across the Little Ring Road from Brussels' core.

Top Three Things To Do North of Center

♦ **Admire rare plants**
Plan your visit to be in town during the three weeks when the **Royal Greenhouses★★** are open.

♦ **Take the kids inside an atom**
You can go inside the "atoms" of the **Atomium★**, a massive model of a molecule of iron crystal, built for Expo '58 *(see Family Fun)*.

♦ **Experience Brussels at its coolest**
From a day spa to a nightclub, you'll find entertainment galore inside the **Tours & Taxis** building *(see Grand Architecture)*.

South of Center, Abbey of Our Lady Of Cambre, Ixelles

MUST SEE

Royal Greenhouses★★

Though they are open only for three weeks a year, the Royal Greenhouses (*see Grand Architecture*) are well worth the detour. During the 19C, progress in construction techniques, especially the use of metal and glass, made a new type of building – the greenhouse – possible. Initially conceived as a vast orangery by William I, the site took on its current look under Léopold II, who asked Belgian architect Alphonse Balat to design a 6-acre complex of glass greenhouses to house his collection of rare plants. Geraniums with leaves the size of an open hand grow along glass-covered walkways, while thousands of bright fuschias hang overhead.

Josaphat Park

A railroad may run through it, but this 20ha/50-acre green haven in the middle of Schaerbeek stands out in a lackluster commune. The park's name is believed to have come from Christian pilgrims, who, upon returning from Palestine, found similarities between the valleys of Roodebeek in Brussels and that of the Josaphat Valley in the Holy Land. Josaphat Park was officially inaugurated in June 1904, with King Léopold II in attendance. A refuge for botanists, owing to the estimated 5,000 trees here, the park is also a joy for walkers (since biking and roller skating are prohibited). In July and August, free concerts are organized on the bandstand.

Place St-Josse

Huddled around this square, the area known as the **Coeur**

Royal Greenhouses of Laeken

© Van Tr-ournont/visitbrussels.be

de St-Josse (the Heart of St. Josse) is worth a wander. For a long time this quarter sat in wait, overshadowed by shopping areas nearby in the city center, but Place St-Josse is fast becoming a shopping destination in its own right. Most of the shops here cluster around the square and connecting streets, in particular, the **Chaussée de Louvain**, thanks to the presence of the discount **Dod** store (*see Shopping*). The Dod location in St-Josse welcomes almost 10,000 shoppers through its doors on many Saturdays. There are also a large number of ethnic bakeries in the vicinity, especially along the Chaussée de Haecht.

SOUTH OF CENTER

Immediately south of the city, the communes of **Ixelles** and **St-Gilles** are a study in contrasts, with some of Brussels' most beautiful Art Nouveau treasures and smart restaurants tucked between more raffish surroundings. Stroll the 2.6km/1.65mi length of **Avenue Louise** (*see Shopping*), a stretch of tony boutiques that extends out from Place Louise. One of Brussels' most beautiful and largest communes, Ixelles straddles both sides of Avenue Louise.

On the east side you'll find the colorful African quarter of **Matongé** as well as the always-on-trend **Place Flagey**, near the serene **Ixelles Ponds** (see Parks and Gardens) and the **Abbey of Our Lady Of Cambre**★★ (See Churches). On the west side of Avenue Louise, Ixelles offers a multitude of restaurants and good shopping on and around **Rue de Bailli**, and a popular market takes place on the **Place du Châtelain**. The upscale neighborhood around **Place Brugmann** (see Shopping for all three) offers a tranquil environment in which to shop and dine, while the adjoining St-Gilles area pulses with students, artists and a thriving immigrant community. On the southern side of Ixelles, the residential commune of **Uccle** boasts one of Brussels' most admired cultural sites, the **David and Alice van Buuren Museum**★★ (see Museums in Greater Brussels).

Top Three Things To Do South of Center

+ **Explore wide-open spaces** Head down Avenue Louise to the **Cambre Woods**★, a vast wooded park laced by paths for walking and biking.

+ **Taste your way through the Châtelain Market** Known for its gourmet-food stalls and its wine bar, the popular market (see Shopping) in the trendy Châtelain area of Ixelles is love at first bite.

+ **Shop on Avenue Louise** You'll recognize the names of the top international designers whose boutiques fan out from the intersection of **Avenue Louise** and Boulevard de Waterloo (see Shopping).

Avenue Louise

Running southeast from Place Louise to the Cambre Woods (the city's largest park), this thoroughfare was commissioned in 1847 to allow easy access to the leafy, wooded park. The avenue, named for King Léopold II's eldest daughter, now boasts some of the chicest addresses in Brussels.

🏛 The Matongé

Porte de Namur is the gateway to this hidden Ixelles neighborhood, named for a marketplace in the city of Kinshasa, Democratic Republic of the Congo. Though Belgium's link to the Congo has a grim history, this area, known for its Congolese population,

---

Hero of the Avenue

Avenue Louise wasn't always an elegant boulevard. Following the German invasion of Belgium during WWII, the Gestapo set up headquarters at nos. 347, 418, 453 and 510. On January 20, 1943, a Brussels-born fighter pilot, **Jean de Sélys Longchamps**, flew his single-seat Hawker Typhoon down Avenue Louise and fired the plane's cannons into number 453. A monument to Longchamps, who received a Distinguished Flying Cross for his daring feat, now stands in front of the building at no. 453 Avenue Louise.

seems plenty joyous. Matongé is home to dozens of nationalities, giving it a multicultural vibe. Head to the pedestrian **Rue Longue Vie** for Indian food, or try to get a table (there are only four) at **Archy's** *(Rue Longue Vie 20)* for Latin American cuisine. Seek out the **Galerie d'Ixelles** *(Chaussée d'Ixelles)* for shops selling African fabrics and other imported goods.

St-Gilles

The first houses in a hamlet outside the city walls called *Obbrussel* (Upper-Brussels) were built between the 7C and the 11C, close to Brussels' highest elevation (100m/328ft). Under French regime, the rural village now known as St-Gilles was hailed for its cabbage cultivation. Today, the town retains its village feel, although it dovetails seamlessly with Brussels. The commune's diverse population is visible at the weekly market at the Parvis de St-Gilles, and in shops such as the Moroccan souk-inspired **La Caravanne Passe** *(Rue de Tamines 2; www.lacaravanepasse.be)*. Home to the Art Nouveau **Horta**

Museum★★ *(see Museums in Greater Brussels)*, St-Gilles also has a large population of students, who frequent the tavern **Moeder Lambic** *(Rue de Savoie 68)*.

EAST OF CENTER

Residential neighborhoods on both sides of the tree-lined Avenue de Tervuren, the communes of **Woluwé-St-Pierre** and **Woluwé-St-Lambert** sit on the east side of the Brussels periphery. Though these tranquil towns are not places to come for a riotous night out, the area is not without its attractions.

Extensive **Woluwé Park** *(see Parks and Gardens)* is a great place to walk and bike; and when it snows, families take to the undulating terrain with their sleds. The **Tram Museum** *(see Family Fun)* intrigues visitors young and old, and the highly acclaimed but little-known **Wittockiana Library**★ *(see Museums in Greater Brussels)* is a bookworm's mecca. For shopping, head to the **Avenue Georges Henri**. The adjacent commune of **Auderghem** plants its feet in the green edges of the 4,421ha/

©Franky De Meyer/iStockphoto

East of Center, Woluwé Park

NEIGHBORHOODS

Ixelles Cemetery

Amid the bars and restaurants surrounding the main campuses of the Université Libre de Bruxelles (ULB) and the Vrije Universiteit Brussels (VUB) you'll find the entrance to this cemetery, hidden behind a brick wall. Several well-known figures are buried here, including architect **Victor Horta**, and French general **George Ernest Boulager**. Boulager sought refuge in Brussels after an attempted coup d'état in Paris in 1889. He committed suicide in 1891 on the tomb of his mistress, Marguerite de Bonnemain, in whose grave he is buried.

10,920-acre **Sonian Forest★★**, the remnants of a much larger ancient forest, where miles of tranquil trails attract outdoorsy types. A visit to the **Red Convent** (see Churches), also located in the forest, offers a different kind of serenity.

Top Three Things To Do East of Center

* **Ride an antique tram**
  On Sundays from April to October, the **Tram Museum** in Woluwé-St-Pierre offers tours in a 1935 tram (see Family Fun).
* **Find out what made Marie so miserable**
  You'd be miserable too if you were buried alive. Find out the whole story at the **Chapel of Marie the Wretched** (see Churches).
* **Spend a day at a lake**
  There's something for everyone in the family to do at the **Mellaerts Ponds**, from fishing and swimming to canoeing and mini-golf (see Parks and Gardens).

Chapel of Marie the Wretched
(Chapelle de Marie-la-Misérable)

This petite chapel in Woluwé-St-Lambert gets its name from a tragic story told by Brussels playwright Michel de Ghelderode (who is interred at **Church of Our Lady of Laeken**; see Churches). The play, called Marie la Misérable, recounts the story of a young peasant girl who rebuffs the advances of a powerful man. To get even and soothe his wounded ego, the seducer slips a valuable vase into Marie's bag, then accuses her of theft. She is unjustly found guilty of the theft and buried alive.

The Woluwé Stream

Running through several communes in the southeastern and eastern parts of Brussels (including Woluwé St-Pierre and Woluwé-St-Lambert), the Woluwé stream is a tributary of the Senne River. Many ponds have formed along the stream over time; two of them, the **Mellaerts Ponds** (see Parks and Gardens) now make a pleasant outing for families. To get a feel for the area, walk along the Woluwé stream, beginning in the park that embraces the **Château Malou** (see Châteaux and Palaces).

WEST OF CENTER

Despite being situated across the Charleroi Canal from Brussels' city center, the western communes of **Molenbeek** and **Anderlecht** don't make many must-go lists.

Molenbeek Lock on the Charleroi Canal
©Rivertours

The municipality of Anderlecht is one of Brussels' largest (1,784ha/ 4,400 acres), known for its football team and as the location of the Midi train station.

Among its museums, Anderlecht counts the **Erasmus House★★**, the **Anderlecht Béquinage** and the **Cantillon Brewery** *(see Museums in Greater Brussels for all three)*.

The **Collegial Church of Saints Peter and Guy★** *(See Churches)* contains the body of St. Guy, a champion of the poor.

Top Three Things To Do West of Center

- ◆ **Shop at the Midi Market** Stock up on North African spices, mint tea and more at this multicultural bazaar.
- ◆ **Introduce yourself to Gueuze** Find out how Brussels' specialty beer is made at the **Cantillon Brewery Museum** *(see Museums in Greater Brussels).*
- ◆ **Cruise the Charleroi Canal** The canal linking Leuven to Mechelen makes an ideal place for a day cruise, while the towpath along the waterway is a good place to bike.

Charleroi Canal

The Charleroi Canal, separating Molenbeek in the west from the Lower Town, was completed in 1827 as a means to transport coal to northern Belgium from the mines of Charleroi. When the industrial activity moved northward in the 20C to the adjoining Canal of Willebroek, Molenbeek declined. Attempts to revitalize the canal area have been talked about for years. Learn more about the canal's history on a boat tour *(www.rivertours.be)*, or rent a bike and ride along the towpath.

Midi Market

If Brussels had a souk, the Midi Market would be it. Early Sunday morning at the Gare du Midi train station, one of Europe's biggest markets unfurls and invites you to feed your senses. By 7am, some 450 stalls are set up to sell food, including North African specialties, olives, cheese, herbs and falafel. In addition to food, kitchenware and clothes are here for the haggling, as is a vast selection of other items like cell-phone covers, purses and tablecloths – all at rock-bottom prices *(see Shopping)*.

HISTORIC SQUARES

The most celebrated square in Brussels, and deservedly so, is the spectacular Grand Place★★★. But tucked behind buildings and hidden on tiny streets are many unassuming "wallflowers" just waiting for their time in the spotlight, many revealing fascinating facets of local history.

🔶 Grand Place★★★

Between Rue de la Tête d'Or and Rue de la Colline, Lower Town. Metro: Gare Centrale or Bourse.

Nothing can prepare you for the first time you see the Grand Place (*place* is the French word for "square"; Grand Place is *de grote Markt* in Dutch), in the opulent heart of Brussels. Tourists bend and contort, trying to fit the grandeur of it into a 2-inch camera screen. It just can't be done. It's best to walk onto the cobblestones and turn 360 degrees to get an overall emotional impression. Over centuries, the sculpted façades here have witnessed the city's pageants and executions, political decrees and food markets. And what draws people to the majestic setting today is what

has attracted them for centuries – the awe-inspiring splendor of the place, designated a UNESCO World Heritage Site in 1998. In the 14C, wealthy family mansions replaced small wooden houses that once dotted the square. Construction of the City Hall and spire began in 1402 (completed in 1420), and other elaborate buildings in a mix of architectural styles (Baroque, Gothic and Louis XIV) were added between the 15C and 16C. The face of the square changed again in 1695, when King Louis XIV of France aimed his cannons at Brussels, razing the Grand Place. Remarkably, the guilds (organizations of the city's craftsmen and merchants) rebuilt the Grand Place in only four years, surrounding the square with striking Baroque-style **Guildhalls★★★** *(opposite)*. Over the years, the Grand Place also changed from a market square into the administrative hub of Brussels, a role it still holds today.

The Guildhalls★★★

Built in 1695, the meeting places for the city's guilds were restored in the 19C. Their Baroque façades surround the Grand Place, many decorated in the three architectural orders – Doric, Ionic and Corinthian. Look up high to see scrolled gables, sculptures, gilded motifs and rich ornamentation.

Guildhalls

©Y. Duhamel/Michelin

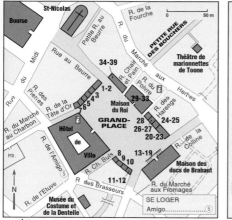

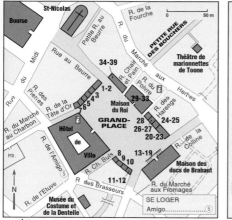

✓ **Manneken Pis**

Numbers refer to the map above.

1–2. Le Roy d'Espagne – The King of Spain's Hall is also called Bakers' Guildhall. There is a bust of Charles II on the façade as well as statues representing energy, water, fire, wind, wheat and prudence, all elements necessary for baking. There's a popular café on the ground floor.

3. La Brouette – Wheelbarrow Hall of the Tallow Merchants' Guild.

4. Le Sac – Sack Hall, once the Guild of Coopers and Cabinet-makers.

5. La Louve – This was the Archers' Guild, named for the sculpture of a she-wolf suckling Romulus and Remus (*la louve* means "she-wolf" in French). The phoenix atop the building symbolizes the structure's two burnings and "rebirths."

6. Le Cornet – A gable shaped like the bow of a 17C frigate marks the Italianate Flemish-style Horn Hall of the Boatmen's Guild.

7. Le Renard – Fox Hall of the Haberdashers' Guild displays

Delicious Streets

The **Grand Place★★★** had humble beginnings as the site of a food market, which is why surrounding streets have names like *beurre* (butter), *herbes* (herbs) and *fromage* (cheese), among others.

Even the ornate **Maison du Roi** (King's House) refers to its origin in its Dutch name, Broodhuis, or Bread House.

bas-relief sculptures of cherubs at work. St. Nicholas, the patron saint of merchants, tops the gable.

8. L'Etoile – Now privately owned, Star Hall was knocked down in 1850 to make way for tourists. So furious was Charles Buls, the mayor at the time, that he had it rebuilt over an arcade. The statue of Everard 't Serclaes is found in the arcade *(see sidebar, p54).*

9. Le Cygne – Today there is a well-known and pricey restaurant inside the Swan Hall of the Butchers' Guild.

HISTORIC SQUARES

10. L'Arbre d'Or – The Brewers' Guild's Golden Tree Hall is crowned by an equestrian statue of Charles of Lorraine, and is the only building on the Grand Place still owned by a guild.

13–19. Maison des Ducs de Brabant – With its golden façade and carved pediment, the House of the Dukes of Brabant contains seven guildhalls. Slender pilasters support busts of the 19 dukes of Brabant.

24–25. La Chaloupe d'Or – The Golden Boat Hall of the Tailors' Guild.

26. Le Pigeon – Writer Victor Hugo stayed in exile in the Pigeon Hall of the Painters' Guild from 1851 to 1852.

28. La Chambrette de l'Amman – The magistrate who represented the Duke of Brabant once occupied the Amman's Garret.

29–33 Maison du Roi
Open Tue–Fri 10am–5pm, Sat–Sun 10am–1pm. €2,50. 02 279 43 55.
The King's House faces the Town Hall and sits on the site of the former Bread Market. It was rebuilt in the 19C. Despite its name, no king has ever stayed here. Today the building houses the **Brussels City Museum** *(see Museums)*.

City Hall (Hôtel de Ville)
Visit by guided tour only. English tours available winter Tue–Wed 3:15pm, summer Tue–Wed 3:15pm & Sun 12:15pm. €2,48. 02 279 43 65. See Grand Architecture.

Place des Martyrs★

On Rue St-Michel, between Rue Neuve and Rue d'Argent, Lower Town. Metro: De Brouckère.

Surrounded by elegant classical houses, this square (formerly the Place de St-Michel) takes its name from the 445 martyrs killed during the fight for Belgian independence in 1830. They are buried underneath the square.

Place du Grand Sablon★

Between Rue des Sablons and Rue Bodenbroek, Lower Town. Metro: Parc or Tram 94 to Petit Sablon.

© Christophe Licoppe/visitbrussels.be

Hôtel de Ville

Considered by many the most beautiful square in Brussels, Place du Grand Sablon is named for the sandy marshes (*sable* is the French word for "sand") that once filled this area. Today the square, surrounded by stately houses, antiques shops and trendy cafés, is crowned by the **Church of Our Lady of Sablon★** (*see Churches*).

Place du Petit Sablon★

Between Rue de la Régence and the Palais d'Egmont, Upper Town. Metro: Parc.

This little square, punctuated by 48 columns topped by bronze statues representing Brussels' medieval guilds, is big on charm. At the far end of the garden, large statues commemorate important people in Belgian history – in particular the counts of **Egmont** and **Hoorns**, who led the Protestant resistance against the Spanish in 1568 and were subsequently beheaded on the Grand Place.

Place Royale★

At the top of Coudenberg Hill, Upper Town. Metro: Parc.

Adjacent to the **Palace of Coudenberg**, cobblestone Place Royale was once a market square. The palace burned down in 1731, and new buildings were erected on the square between 1773 and 1780. In the center of the Place Royale stands a statue of Godfrey of Bouillon, leader of the first crusade in 1096. On the square you'll also discover the **Church of St. Jacques on Coudenberg** (*see Churches*) and the wildly popular **Magritte Museum★★** (*see Museums*).

Place du Petit Sablon

©Olivier van de Kerchove/visitbrussels.be

Place Poelaert

At the south end of Rue de la Régence, Upper Town. Metro: Louise or Tram 94 to Poelaert.

This square lies atop what was once "Gallows Hill," where the bodies of executed criminals hung on a gibbet as an example to other would-be wrong-doers. Overlooking the square, the **Palace of Justice** (*see Grand Architecture*) was designed by the square's namesake, Joseph Poelaert. From here, an extensive view stretches over Brussels.

🦁 Place St-Géry

Between Rue d'Anderlecht and Boulevard Anspach, Lower Town. Metro: Bourse.

St-Géry now ranks as the nightlife hub in the capital, but centuries ago, the square was the site of Brussels' first settlement, founded in the 6C on an island in the Senne River. A former market hall turned exhibition space, **Les Halles de St-Géry** dominates the square.

HISTORIC SQUARES

GRAND ARCHITECTURE

From Baroque and Flemish Renaissance splendor to the sinuous curves and floral motifs of Art Nouveau and the quirky design of modern structures like the **Atomium★**, Belgium's capital shows off a richness of architectural styles. Even if you're not a student of architecture, you can't help admiring the striking buildings all around you.

Galeries St-Hubert★★

Between Rue Marché aux Herbes and Rue de L'Ecuyer, Lower Town. Metro: Gare Centrale.
See Shopping.

Now filled with shops, the elegant classical gallery on the Grand Place was built in 1846 according to plans by J.P. Cluysenaar. Note the glazed vaults supported by an elegant metal framework on Neoclassical **Galerie du Roi** and **Galerie de la Reine**.
The latter crosses **Rue des Bouchers★** and leads into the **Galerie des Princes**, which opens onto Rue de l'Ecuyer. Galeries St-Hubert is a fine example of the covered shopping arcades built in the 19C, and is only one of three

that remain in Brussels (along with the adjacent Renaissance-style **Galerie Bortier**, and the Northern Passage, near Rue Neuve.

Royal Greenhouses of Laeken★★
(Serres royales de Laeken)

Avenue du Parc Royale 61, Laeken. Metro: Heysel. Open three weeks in Apr–May. €2. 02 513 89 40. www.monarchie.be.

This remarkable complex of eleven linked 19C iron and glass greenhouses is located in the park surrounding the **Royal Castle of Laeken**. Though they are only open for three weeks each spring, it's worth the effort to plan to see them. King Léopold II, his architect, Alphonse Balat, and an architecture student named Victor Horta all had a hand in designing the veritable palaces of glass that harbor many varieties of flora and rare plants collected from the Congo.

Atomium★

Boulevard du Centenaire, Atomium Square, Heysel. Metro: Heysel. Open year-round daily 10am–6pm (last admission at 5:30pm). €11. 02 475 47 77. www.atomium.be.
See Family Fun.

An icon on the Brussels skyline, the 102m/34ft-high Atomium dominates the Heysel plateau

Atomium

©www.atomium.be - SABAM 2009 - Frankinho

MUST SEE

National Basilica of the Sacred Heart

©Julian Love/Apa Publications

as a relic of the 1958 World's Fair. Architect André Waterkeyn designed the space-age structure to represent an iron crystal enlarged 165 billion times. It took roughly 18 months to build, and the nine spheres – each with a diameter of 18m/59ft – are linked by tubes through which visitors can move from one sphere to the next. A permanent exhibit in the lowest sphere catalogs Expo '58 through painstakingly re-created models of 27 of the fair's pavilions. An elevator will whisk you to the topmost sphere for a panoramic view over Brussels.

National Basilica of the Sacred Heart★
(Basilique Nationale du Sacré-Coeur)

Parvis de la Basilique1, Koekelberg. Metro: Simonis. Open summer 9am –5:15pm, winter 10am–4:15pm. €4. 02 421 16 69. www.basilique.be. See Churches.

Its green copper dome rising 90m/295ft above Koekelberg Hill, this vast basilica took 65 years (1905–1970) to complete. The Catholic basilica is the fifth-largest church and the largest Art Deco building in the world. Architect

A River Ran Through It

Like most other major European cities, Brussels has a river coursing through its center. However, Brussels' river, the Senne (Zenne), is underground, bricked over intentionally in the 1860s and 70s.

Brussels' main waterway grew more polluted as the city grew and eventually became a health hazard. To stem the tide of the polluted waterway that inundated Lower Town every time the river flooded – which was frequently – Mayor Jules Anspach approved a city beautification plan in 1865. The plan, conceived by architect Léon Suys, called for covering the Senne and creating a series of grand boulevards and public buildings (**The Bourse** among them) over it.

Today the only place in Brussels where you can still see the Senne River below the city is at **La Grande Écluse** (The Great Lock) restaurant, housed in a 19C building near the Gare du Midi train station *(Boulevard Poincaré 77; 02 522 30 25; www.grande-ecluse.be).*

Manneken Pis★★

Corner of Rue de l'Etuve and Rue du Chêne, Upper Town. A few hundred meters away from the **Grand Place★★★**, this Cupid-like statue is famous for its cheeky charm. It was sculpted in 1619 by Jérôme Duquesnoy the Elder, and once provided the district's water supply. The tradition of dressing the statue began in 1698 when the governor of the Netherlands gave the city a blue wool coat for the chubby naked bronze boy. Since then, almost every country has made a contribution to the statue's wardrobe, which takes up an entire room in the **Brussels City Museum** *(see Museums)*.

Albert Van Huffel designed the reinforced-concrete structure using glazed terra-cotta as the framework.

Anneessens Tower
(Tour Anneessens)

Boulevard de l'Empereur, below the Place du Grand Sablon, Lower Town. Metro: Gare Centrale.

Restored in 1967, this corner tower is a relic of the first city wall (11C–13C). The tower, with its octagonal staircase, rests on two broken barrel-vaulted floors. The tower's namesake, a man named Anneessens, represented the tradesmen rebelling against the Austrian government. He was supposedly imprisoned here before his execution in 1719.

The Bourse

Rue de la Bourse, Lower Town. Metro: Bourse. Guided tours depart from the Hôtel de Ville the first Wed of the month at 11:15am. 02 279 43 55.

The stately building that houses the Brussels Stock Exchange does not have a formal name; it is simply called The Bourse (the French term for stock exchange). Built between 1868 and 1873, the

Neoclassical structure designed by Léon Suys resembles the Paris Opera. The myriad ornamentation and sculptures that decorate The Bourse were created by a number of famous sculptors, including French artist Albert-Ernest Carrier-Belleuse and his assistant at the time, a young artist named Auguste Rodin.

Chinese Pavilion and Japanese Tower
(Pavillon chinois et Tour japonais)

Avenue Van Praet 44, Laeken. Tram 3 or 7: Pavillon chinois. Open Tue–Fri 9:30am–5pm, Sat–Sun 10am–5pm. €4 (free first Wed of the month after 1pm). 02 268 16 08. www.kmkg-mrah.be.

After a visit to the 1900 Universal Exhibition in Paris, King Léopold II had the park surrounding his palace decorated with exotic monuments. The Japanese Tower (1904) and the Chinese Pavilion (1909) resulted from this plan. Designed by architect Alexandre Marcel, the tower incorporates the reconstructed porch from the 1900 World's Fair in Paris, while the latter displays ornate outer wooden paneling imported from Shanghai. Today they house the

MUST SEE

Museums of the Far East (see
Museums in Greater Brussels).

City Hall
(Hôtel de Ville)

*On the Grand Place, Lower Town.
Metro: Gare Centrale or Bourse.
Visit by guided tour only. English
tours available winter Tue–Wed
3:15pm, summer Tue–Wed 3:15pm
& Sun 12:15pm. Closed Mon &
public holidays. €2,48. 02 279 43 65.*

A marvel of daring elegance by
Van Ruysbroeck, Brussels' City Hall
was completed in 1455 on the
awe-inspiring **Grand Place★★★**
(see Historic Squares); today it is
considered one of Belgium's finest
civic buildings. Stop to admire the
hall's symmetry, the 137 sculptures
carved into the exterior walls, and
the lovely Gothic tower. Its spire,
which escaped unscathed during
King Louis XIV's attack on Brussels
in 1695, is topped by the archangel
St. Michael. Tours of the interior
reveal tapestries from the 16C–18C
as well as precious paintings and
ornate rooms.

Congress Column
(Colonne du Congrès)

*Place de la Liberté, Rue du Congrès,
Upper Town. Metro: Madou.*

This 47m/154ft-tall monument
commemorates the formation of
the Belgian state and signing of
the constitution by the National
Congress in 1830–1831. Erected in
1859, the monument was designed
by Joseph Poelaert and is capped
by a statue of King Léopold I. At the
foot of the column is a memorial
to the Belgian victims of WWI and
the tomb of the unknown soldiers,
flanked by an eternal flame.

Halle Gate

©Olivier van de Kerchove/visitbrussels.be

Halle Gate
(Porte de Hal)

*Boulevard du Midi, St-Gilles.
Metro: Porte de Hal. Open Tue–Fri
9:30am–5pm, Sat–Sun 10am–5pm.
Closed Mon. €5. 02 534 15 18.
www.kmkg-mrah.be.*

This 600-year-old turreted tower,
which looks like it was plucked
from a fairy tale, is the last
surviving remnant of Brussels'
second wall and was one of the
seven entry gates to the medieval
city. It now contains a small
museum dedicated to Brussels'
medieval history.

Old England
Department Store

*Rue Montagne de la Cour, Upper
Town. Metro: Parc.*

Designed by Belgian architect Paul
Saintenoy, the splendid 1899 **Old
England Department Store** in
Mont des Arts shows off one of the
finest examples of the Art Nouveau
style. The store was once a shop
catering to well-to-do Brussels
women; now it holds the **Museum**

Old England Department Store

Palace of Justice
(Palais de Justice)

Place Poelaert, Upper Town. Metro: Louise. Open year-round Mon–Fri 9am–4pm. Closed weekends.

Built between 1860 and 1880 by Joseph Poelaert, the enormous edifice is believed to have been the world's largest building constructed in the 19C. The dimensions of the palace are awesome: it is 105m/340ft high and covers a total surface of 24,000m²/258,000sq ft. The palace still functions as the supreme court of law for the country of Belgium.

Parliament Building
(Palais de la Nation)

Rue de la Loi 16, Upper Town. Metro: Parc. Open to the public when Parliament is in session, Mon–Sat 10am–3pm. 02 519 81 36. www.fed-parl.be.

Facing Brussels Park opposite the Royal Palace, this splendid

of Musical Instruments★★★ *(see Museums)*. With its six floors of glass and curving metal, the former department store building is one of the city's most recognizable structures.

©ARCO/De Meester/age fotostock

Art Nouveau

Brussels boasts a rich Art Nouveau heritage, with some 500 buildings and façades, cafés and bars that illustrate this revolutionary architectural style. Marked by ornate curling ironwork, rounded windows, stained glass, and curving details down to the doorknobs, the Art Nouveau style is everywhere, if you know where to look:

- With its ornate decoration, the **Maison de St-Cyr** (Cyr House) on Place Ambiorix is one of the most beautiful homes in the city.
- The 1893 **Maison Autrique** (Autrique House; *Chaussée de Haecht 266*) was the first town house built by Victor Horta, a master of the Art Nouveau style.
- The airy **Waucquez Warehouses**, also designed by Horta, house the **Belgian Centre for Comic Strip Art★★** *(see Museums)*.
- **Hotel Metropole**'s *(see Must Stay)* stunning interior and stained-glass windows are a true celebration of the style.
- Stunning Art Nouveau details highlight the interior of **Le Falstaff** *(Rue Henri Maus 19)*, a popular brasserie.

Neoclassical structure was designed by architect Barnabé Guimard and built in 1779, when Maria-Theresa of Austria took the throne. Since 1830, however, it has been the home of Belgium's Parliament. Guided tours can be arranged in advance by telephone and are conducted when Parliament is not in session.

SQUARE
(Palais des Congrès)

Rue Mont des Arts, Upper Town. Metro: Gare Centrale. 02 515 13 18. www.square-brussels.com.

You can't miss this giant modular cube on the Brussels cityscape. The extensive conference center is housed in the former Palais des Congrès – the architecturally significant edifice erected for the 1958 World's Fair. Many of the original features, including murals by Paul Delvaux, René Magritte and Louis van Lint, have been carefully restored and provide a striking contrast to the contemporary design of SQUARE.

Tour & Taxis Building

Avenue du Port, 86c, Schaerbeek. Metro: Ribaucourt. Hours vary. 02 420 60 69. www.tourtaxis.be.

This urban retail and event space takes up a 1097 customs warehouse with a long history in Brussels. The name derives from the **von Thurn und Thassis** family, a celebrated European dynasty and founders of the European postal service, who used this land bordering the port as horse pastures. On the building's façade you'll see the coats of arms of Belgian cities and provinces.

The interior is bathed in natural light, and with varying textures of brick, glass, and steel, encasing 57,000 m²/643,542sq ft of space. A central pathway still shows traces of a railway that once ran through the building. Major exhibitions, offices, and retail customers now call Tour & Taxis home. Each June, the **Couleur Café** music festival takes place here *(see Calendar of Events)*.

Triumphal Arch

Between Rue de la Loi and Avenue Tervuren, Upper Town. Metro: Mérode or Schuman.

Second in size only to the Arc de Triomphe in Paris, this monumental arch symbolizes the economic and industrial strength of Belgium and marks the entrance to **Cinquantenaire Park**. In 1880, Belgium celebrated 50 years of independence, and King Léopold II was keen to have a world exhibition in Brussels. The stately monument also served as the entrance gate to Brussels for people approaching via the newly laid Avenue de Tervuren. The arch wasn't finished until 1905, about 25 years too late for the 50th anniversary, but just in time for the 75th. Bookending the arch are the gorgeous **Bordiau Halls** (named for the architect Jules Bordiau), which display the glass and iron construction that was so popular in late-19C Europe.

MUSEUMS

Brussels is famed for many things, such as culinary gems like mussels, chocolate and beer. But culture vultures might be surprised to learn the city claims more than 100 museums showcasing a variety of themes, encompassing art and architecture, history, comics, science, cinema and more.

Cinquantenaire Museum★★★
(Musée du Cinquantenaire)

Cinquantenaire Park, Upper Town. Metro: Mérode or Schuman. Open Tue–Fri 9:30am–5pm, Sat–Sun & public holidays 10am–5pm. Closed public holidays. €5 (free first Wed of the month after 1pm). 02 741 72 11. www.kmkg-mrah.be.

Touring Tip

Attention museum lovers: consider purchasing a **Brussels Card**, which includes free entry to more than 30 museums plus access to public transportation *(www.brusselscard.be; see Practical Information).*

A collection of diplomatic gifts and royal mementos first displayed in the Royal Arsenal, the core of this museum harkens back to the 15C. Holdings today feature a wide range of artifacts and antiquities from Asia, Egypt and the Middle East, as well as decorative arts from all periods.

Antiquities from the civilizations of Palestine, Cyprus and Mesopotamia fill the ground floor. Exhibits cover Ancient Rome, Etruria and Greece. The great colonnade of Apamea has been reconstructed here as a reminder of the Belgian missions in Syria. Egypt is also featured with one of the oldest Books of the Dead; the **Dame de Bruxelles**, a statue dating to 2600 BC; and the striking bas-relief representing **Queen Tiy**, wife of Amenhotep III.

The **America Rooms** contain splendid collections of pre-Columbian and ethnographic art, while the gallery devoted to decorative arts from the Middle Ages to the Baroque period contains

Cinquantenaire Museum

©Musées royaux d'Art et d'Histoire

some exquisite **tapestries**. Also here is the **St. George Altarpiece** by Jan Borman the Elder (1493), which stands out among the wooden **retables** for its lifelike figures. Archaeological objects take in the reconstruction of a Roman dwelling, as well as tools, pottery and jewelry uncovered during digs in Belgium.

Museum of Ancient Art★★★
(Musée d'Art ancien)

Rue de la Régence 3, Upper Town. Métro: Parc. Open Tue–Sun 10am–5pm. Closed Mon & public holidays. €5 (includes Museum of Modern Art); free first Wed of the month after 1pm. 02 508 32 11. www.finearts-museum.be.

Opened in 1887, the museum is famous throughout the world for its outstanding collection of Flemish art and Old Masters, spanning the period from the 15C–18C. Works are presented in chronological order so visitors can view the evolution of pictorial art. One of the museum's oldest paintings is *Scenes From the Life of the Virgin Mary* by an anonymous master from the Southern Low Countries (late 14C). The work of the Tournai painter **Rogier**

Museum of Ancient Art

©Y. Duhamel/Michelin

van der Weyden is represented by portraits such as *Antoine, Great Bastard of Burgundy* and *Laurent Froimont*, both marvels of simplicity, and by a magnificent *Pietà*. Other works include **Hans Memling**'s tender *Virgin and Child* and *Calvary With Donor* by **Hieronymus Bosch**. **Gérard David**, the last of the great Primitive painters, is represented by *Virgin With Milk Soup*. Room 31 is a shrine to **Bruegel the Elder**. *The Fall of the Rebel Angels* shows the influence Hieronymus Bosch had on Bruegel at the beginning of his career. Representing the **17C and 18C**, works by **Peter-Paul Rubens**

The Royal Belgian Museum of Fine Arts★★★
The Museum of Ancient Art is actually part of the Royal Belgian Museum of Fine Arts (Musées royau des Beaux-Arts de Belgique), which also comprises the **Museum of Modern Art★★**, the **Constantine Meunier Museum★** and the **Wiertz Museum**. You can move freely between the Museum of Ancient Art and the Museum of Modern Art, which are located in the main building near the **Place Royale★**. The other two institutions are much smaller, dedicated to specific Belgian artists, and are located in a separate building a few kilometers from the city center.

MUSEUMS

include *Adoration of the Magi*, *Ascent to Calvary* and *Martyrdom of St. Livinus*, as well as some of his more personal works (*Negro Heads* and *Portrait of Hélène Fourment*). **Jordaens**, **Van Dyck**, **Teniers** and **Frans Hals** are also featured.

Museum of Musical Instruments★★★
(Musées des Instruments de Musique)

Rue Montagne de la Cour 2, Upper Town. Metro: Parc. Open year-round daily 9:30am–5pm, Sat–Sun 10am–5pm (last admission at 4:15pm). €5 (free first Wed of the month after 1pm). 02 545 01 30. www.mim.fgov.be.

Now located in the duo of **Old England Department Store** buildings (1899) on **Place Royale★** – an Art Nouveau edifice and a Neoclassical gem – this marvel of a museum began in 1877 when it was attached to the Brussels Royal Music Conservatory.

MIM's collection of more than 7,000 musical instruments from around the world is a joy for young and old alike. Hurdy-gurdies, accordions, drums and instruments used in the Chinese opera represent some of the folk instruments that spread over several floors. And you can listen to many of them via headphones. One section of the museum is devoted to Adolphe Sax *(see sidebar, below)*.

The café under the glass dome on the top floor is a great place to take a break, while the gift shop is a treasure trove of books, games and musical gadgets.

Autoworld★★

Cinquantenaire Park, Upper Town. Metro: Mérode or Schuman. Open Apr–Sept 10am–6pm; Oct–Mar 10am–5pm. €6. 02 736 41 65. www.autoworld.be.

Car lovers, take note: some 450 vehicles, mostly cars, are displayed beneath the high glass roof of the south hall of the Palais du Cinquantenaire. The story of the automobile is told in detail here, partly through a group of vehicles that belonged to prestigious collector and enthusiast **Ghislain Mahy**. The Belgian makes – including examples from Belga Rise, Hermès, Imperia, Miesse, Nagant and Vivinus – deserve particular attention. There are also vehicles from **Sylvain de Jong**, who founded Minerva Motors in Antwerp in 1883.

Bugle Boy

Everyone has heard of the jazzy instrument called the saxophone, but did you know that the name "Sax" could be traced back to a tiny town in Belgium? **Antoine-Joseph "Adolphe" Sax** was born in **Dinant★★** *(see Excursions)* in 1814. The son of an accomplished instrument maker, Sax worked for his father making improvements to the clarinet and bass clarinet. In 1841, he relocated to Paris and began work on a new set of instruments – valve bugles – which were exhibited there in 1844. Though Sax did not invent them, his more sophisticated examples of valve bugles quickly became known as saxhorns. The instrument for which Adolphe Sax is now best known, the saxophone, was patented in 1846.

Belgian Center for Comic Strip Art★★
(Centre Belge de la Bande Dessinée)

Rue des Sables 20, Lower Town. Metro: Gare Centrale. Open year-round Tue–Sun 10am–6pm. Closed Mon. €8. 02 219 19 80. www.cbbd.be.

Belgium's temple to comic-strip art is housed in a 1903 Art Nouveau building called the **Waucquez Warehouses**, designed by Victor Horta. The vast entrance hall contains a bookshop, a library and a restaurant. **Birth of a Comic Strip** explains how comic strips are conceived and follows the process through to the finished product. In the **Treasury**, you'll discover a collection of more than 3,000 original plates by the greatest comic-strip writers of all time. The **Museum of the Imagination** immerses you in the world of the great heroes of Belgian comic strips and their creators from Tintin (Hergé) to the Smurfs (Peyo), while the **Gallery** looks at the development of this art form in more modern times.

Tintin Live

Tintin fans, take note: at the end of 2011, Tintin will come alive on the silver screen thanks to director Steven Spielberg and actors Jamie Bell (Tintin), Andy Serkis (Captain Haddock) and Daniel Craig (Red Rackham).

Magritte Museum★★
(Musée Magritte)

Place Royale 1–2, Upper Town. Metro: Parc. Open Tue–Sun 10am–5pm (Wed until 8pm). Closed Mon & public holidays. €8 (€13, combination with museums of Modern Art and Ancient Art). 02 508 32 11. www.musee-magritte-museum.be.

Without a doubt, the Magritte Museum ranks as one of Brussels' star attractions since its opening in 2009. The museum, set up in chronological order over three levels following different periods in the artist's life, boasts the world's richest collection devoted to Belgian Surrealist **René Magritte** (1898–1967). More than 200 works

Belgian Center for Comic Strip Art

MUSEUMS

by Magritte are housed here, encompassing oils on canvas, gouaches, drawings, sculptures and painted objects, as well as advertising posters, musical scores, and vintage photographs and films shot by Magritte himself. Book your tickets online to avoid long lines or disappointment at the entrance. See more Magritte works in the commune of Jette (see p75).

Museum of Modern Art★★
(Musée d'Art moderne)

Access from Place Royale, Upper Town. Metro: Parc. Open Tue–Sun 10am–5pm. Closed Mon & public holidays. €5 (includes Museum of Ancient Art); free first Wed of the month after 1pm. 02 508 32 11. www.finearts-museum.be.

Opened in 1984, the Museum of Modern Art houses 19C painting and sculpture collections, and 20C statues, paintings and drawings. Eight of the museum's levels are underground, but a large light well allows many of the works to be seen in natural light.

The **19C section** covers **Neo-classicism** (Jacques-Louis David, *Death of Marat*), **Romanticism**, **Realism** and **Luminism** (*Portrait* of *Jenny Montigny* by Émile Claus). **Symbolism** is represented by **Fernand Khnopff** with *Portrait of Marguerite*, *Memories* and the enigmatic *Carresses*. French Impressionist and neo-Impressionist works include paintings by Gauguin, Vuillard, Seurat and Bonnard (*Nu à contre-jour*), along with Rodin's famous statue *The Thinker*.

Level 3 devotes itself to **contemporary art** and presents white, life-sized sculptures by Georges Segal, works by Anselm Kiefer (*Bérénice*, 1989), Henry Moore, Pol Bury, Nam June Paik, Sam Francis, Claes Oldenburg and Francis Bacon. Of particular interest are works by **Rik Wouters** (*Lady in Blue Before Mirror*, 1912; *Flute Player*, 1914). The museum also displays Abstract art and works by the Belgian **Futurists** (Jules Schmalzigaug and Prosper de Troyer) and the members of **CoBrA** (Pierre Alechinsky, Karel Appel). Works by Delvaux and Magritte illustrate the importance of Surrealism and Symbolism in 19C Belgium.

The **Georgette and René Magritte Room** displays works such as *The Man of the Sea*, *Midnight Marriage*, *Empire of Lights*, *The Secret Gambler*, *Black Magic Pebble* and *Arnhem Domain*.

Royal Museum of Natural Sciences★★
(Muséum des Sciences Naturelles, Institut Royal)

Rue Vautier 29, Upper Town. Metro: Maalbeek. Open Tue–Sun 9:30am–4:45pm, Sat–Sun & school holidays (except Jul–Aug) 10am–6pm. Closed Mon & public

In His Own Words

"My painting is visible images which conceal nothing; they evoke mystery and, indeed, when one sees one of my pictures, one asks oneself this simple question: 'What does that mean?' It does not mean anything, because mystery means nothing either, it is unknowable." – René Magritte

Palace of Brussels Past

Enter through BELvue (above).
The main residence of King
Charles V and a seat of power
in Europe for six centuries, the
former **Coudenberg Palace**
(see Châteaux And Palaces). is
now a major archaeological site
and museum in the center of
Brussels. Excavations in the 1990s
uncovered large portions of the
ancient ruins, which date to 1100.

holidays. €7. 02 627 42 38.
www.sciencesnaturelles.be.
See Family Fun.

BELvue Museum★
(Musée BELvue)

Place des Palais 7, Upper Town.
Metro: Parc. Open Tue–Fri 10am–
5pm, Sat–Sun 10am–6pm.
Closed Mon, Jan 1 & Dec 25. €5;
€8 combination ticket with Palace
of Coudenberg. 07 022 04 92.
www.belvue.be.

Opened as a luxury hotel in
1777, the **Hôtel de Belle-Vue**
(see sidebar, p83) became part of
the Royal Palace in the 20C and
was the residence of Princess
Clémentine, daughter of Léopold
II. Today, as a museum, the
house offers visitors a glimpse
of the Belgian dynasty, from the
revolution in 1830 to the present,
via photos, letters, paintings and
mementos. The **King Baudouin
Memorial** is devoted to a
monarch beloved by the people
of Belgium. You can access the
remains of the former **Palace
of Coudenbourg** below the
museum.

Charlier Museum★
(Musée Charlier)

Avenue des Arts 16, Upper Town.
Metro: Arts-Loi and Madou.
Open Mon–Thu noon–5pm, Fri
10am–1pm. Closed weekends &
public holidays. €5. 02 218 53 82.
www.charliermusem.be.

This museum reveals the treasures
of wealthy art collector **Henri
van Cutsem** who purchased
the buildings in 1890. After
combining the two façades, van
Cutsem commissioned his friend
architect **Victor Horta** to design
the glass roof in order to provide
natural light for his collections.
He then invited the sculptor/artist
Guillaume Charlier (1854-1925)
to move in. Charlier, the sole heir
to his patron's estate, inherited the
mansion and commissioned Victor
Horta to design a museum to
show off van Cutsem's impressive
collection of paintings ranging
from the late 19C to the 20C.

©Serge Bresson/Charlier Museum

Charlier Museum

Cauchie House★
(Maison Cauchie)

Rue des Francs 5, Upper Town. Metro: Mérode. Open the first Sat & Sun of each month 11am–1pm and 2pm–6pm. €4. 02 673 15 06.

The home of architect and decorative artist **Paul Cauchie** (1875–1952) dates from 1905. If you can't access the museum owing to its limited hours, at least pass by the front to see the *sgraffito*, a technique similar to fresco painting, which decorates the façade.

🍺 Belgian Brewers Museum
(Musée de la Brasserie)

Brewers' House, Grand Place 10, Lower Town. Metro: Gare Centrale or Bourse. Open daily from 10am–5pm. €5. 02 511 49 87. www.beerparadise.be.

Tucked in the vaults of the Brewers' House (Maison des Brasseurs) on the Grand Place, the museum takes visitors through an old pub and brewery full of antique tankards and paraphernalia. You'll also see the process of beer-making, from the raw materials (water, malt, hops, yeast) to a modern brewing hall where computer science aids the master brewers. Of course, a sample of beer awaits at the tour's end.

Brussels City Museum
(Musée de la ville de Bruxelles)

Grand Place (facing the Town Hall), Lower Town. Metro: Gare Centrale or Bourse. Open year-round Tue–Fri 10am–5pm, Sat–Sun 10am–1pm. Closed Mon. €3. 02 279 43 55. www.brucity.be.

The contents of this museum, located in the stunning **King's House** (Maison du Roi), are dedicated to the city's history and the life of its inhabitants over the centuries, as depicted in sculptures, tapestries, altarpieces and models of the city of Brussels. The original version of Brussels' most famous resident, the **Manneken Pis★★** *(see sidebar, p59)*, is carefully preserved here along with his extensive wardrobe gifted from dignitaries around the world.

Cinematek

Palais des Beaux Arts. Rue Baron Horta 9, Upper Town. Metro: Parc or Gare Centrale. Doors open Mon, Tue & Fri 4:30pm, Wed, Sat & Sun 2:30pm, Thu 12:30pm. €3. 02 551 19 19. www.cinematek.be.

Cinematek traces the early stages of the silver screen and showcases the inventions and equipment that led to the development of cinematography between the 18C and 19C. Located in the

---

Catch the Fever

02 512 77 80. www.museumnightfever.be. Each year (in late February or early March), more than 20 Brussels museums stay open late and host a variety of activities during **Museum Night Fever**. From concerts and performances to fashion shows and guided tours, a wide array of events ensure that a night at the museum is a night to remember. Free shuttles take you between the various museums. Get your tickets early, as this event sells out quickly.

Cinematek

BOZAR complex *(see Performing Arts)*, the museum owns more than 60,000 films and a library of 50,000 volumes – not to mention the collection of cinematographic equipment. An on-site movie theater screens weekly silent films with live piano accompaniment – a real retro treat for cinema buffs.

Costume and Lace Museum
(Musée du Costume et de la Dentelle)

Rue de la Violette 12, Lower Town. Metro: Gare Centrale. Open Mon–Tue & Thu–Fri, 10am–12:30pm & 1:30pm–5pm, Sat–Sun 2pm–5pm. Closed Wed & public holidays. €3. 02 279 44 50.

This small museum presents costumes, lacework, embroidery, antique lace, accessories and documents from the 18C to the 20C. Laid out in drawers and neat displays, the beautiful collection contains lace made on the spindle and with needles, not only from Brussels but also from France and Italy.

Marc Sleen Foundation

Rue des Sables 33-35, Lower Town. Metro: Botanique. Open Tue–Sun 11am–1pm, 2pm–4pm. Closed Mon. €2,50. 02 219 19 80. www.marc-sleen.be.

Opened in 2009, located across the street from the **Belgian Center for Comic Strip Art★★**, the Marc Sleen Foundation is both a museum and a memory vault honoring master comic-strip artist and brilliant cartoonist Marc Sleen, best known for creating *The Adventures of Nibbs* (Nero in Flemish). Here visitors will find a reading room, drawings, and a series of temporary exhibits. All text and descriptions are labeled in French, Dutch and English.

Museum Bruxella 1238
(Musée Bruxella 1238)

Rue de la Bourse, Lower Town (to the left of The Bourse). Metro: Bourse. Guided tour in English first Wed of month, 10:15am (call to reserve). €4. 02 279 43 50.

If archaeology turns you on, head for this 1238 Franciscan friary, now

MUSEUMS

a specialized archaeological site. Here you'll find the remains of the original church, monastery and burial vaults.

Museum of Cocoa and Chocolate
(Musée de Cacao et du Chocolat)

Rue de la Tête, Lower Town. Metro: Bourse or Gare Centrale. Open Tue–Sun 10am–4:30pm. €5,50. 02 514 20 48. www.mucc.be. See Family Fun.

Museum of the 18th Century
(Palace of Charles of Lorraine)

Place du Musée 1 (northwest side), Upper Town. Metro: Parc. Open Wed & Sat 1pm–5pm. Closed Sun–Tue, Thu, public holidays & last week of Dec. €3. 02 519 53 11.

The Neoclassical apartments of **Charles of Lorraine**, Governor General of the Austrian

Netherlands (1744–1780), occupy the only surviving wing of his former palace. Five rooms display 18C objects, illustrating the life of aristocrats in the Austrian Netherlands and the court of Brussels during this time. Highlights include the marvelous rotunda with its rosette-patterned floor made from 28 different types of Belgian marble, and the striking staircase that holds a statue of Hercules sculpted by Laurent Delvaux.

Museum of the National Bank of Belgium
(Musée de la Banque nationale de Belgique)

Rue du Bois Sauvage 10, Lower Town. Metro: Gare Centrale. Open Tue–Sun 10am–6pm. Closed Mon. €5 (free first Wed of the month after 1pm). 02 221 22 06. www.nbbmuseum.be.

Money never sleeps here. Housed in a stunning 1872 building, the former home of the Union du Crédit de Bruxelles, this museum invites visitors to follow the money trail through exhibits that explore the world of the mint. It examines ancient forms of payment, the history of money minting, the development of the Euro, money's role in economy, forgeries and more.

Museum of the National Bank of Belgium

©Museum of the National Bank of Belgium

MUST SEE

Royal Library of Belgium
(Bibliothèque royale de Belgique)

Boulevard de l'Empereur 4, Lower Town. Metro: Gare Centrale. Open to readers with pre-booked membership cards, Mon–Fri 9am–1pm & 2pm–5pm. Closed Sun, public holidays & last week in Aug. €5. 02 519 53 57. www.kbr.be.

The Albert I Royal Library was founded in the 15C during the reign of the Dukes of Burgundy. Open to the public since 1839, the library's collection numbers some four million volumes, manuscripts, prints and drawings, maps, coins and medallions. Considered one of the most important cultural institutions in Belgium, this library in the Mont des Arts district is the depository for all books ever published in Belgium or abroad by Belgian authors. Here you'll also find the **Museum of Literature**, a **Printing Museum**, and the 1520 **Chapel of Nassau**, now used for temporary exhibitions. The **Printing Museum** displays machines and printing presses, illustrating the art of bookbinding.

Royal Museum of the Armed Forces and Military History
(Musée Royal de l'Armée et Histoire Militaire)

Parc du Cinquantenaire, Upper Town. Metro: Mérode or Schuman. Open Feb–Dec, Tue–Sun 9am–noon & 1pm–4:30pm. 02 737 79 07. www.museedelarmee.be.

Fans of military history will find much to interest them here. The museum illustrates the country's military history from 1789 to the

Royal Museum of the Armed Forces and Military History

©Franky De Meyer/iStockphoto

present with a **collection of arms and armor★**, and the superb **Titeca et Ribaucourt collection★** of weapons and helmets. Kids will enjoy the **Air and Space section★**, where they can climb into a cargo plane and play pilot in a fighter jet. The 100 planes displayed here range from a little Nieuport, one of the mainstays of France's air force in World War I, to a British Spitfire from World War II. The museum's tank and armored-vehicle sections will reopen in 2012.

The Wiertz Museum
(Musée Wiertz)

Rue Vautier 62, Upper Town. Metro: Schuman. Open year-round daily 10am–12pm & 1pm–5pm. 02 648 17 18.

Located near Park Léopold, behind the European Parliament building, this museum is devoted to the particular universe of Belgian painter and sculptor **Antoine-Joseph Wiertz** (1806–1865), an important figure in the Belgian Romantic Movement. His large-scale canvasses often depicted dramatic and disturbing scenes.

MUSEUMS

MUSEUMS IN GREATER BRUSSELS

If you don't mind leaving the center of the city, there is a wealth of cultural institutions in the outlying area. Depending on your interests, you'll find everything from rare books to rare brews covered in museums that definitely merit a visit if time permits.

David and Alice van Buuren Museum★★
(Musée David et Alice van Buuren)

Avenue Leo Errera 41, Uccle. Tram 3, 23 or 24: Churchill. Open year-round Wed–Mon 2pm–5:30pm. €10. 02 343 48 51. www.museumvanbuuren.com.

Art patrons and philanthropists, David and Alice van Buuren used the funds from the fortune David made in the financial services industry to build this magnificent Art Deco house in the Uccle neighborhood of Brussels. Though born in Gouda, Holland, in 1886, van Buuren eventually settled in Brussels, where he met and married Alice Piette. Over a period of 30 years, the couple turned their home and garden into a living gallery, filled with a magnificent collection of antique furniture, fine carpets, stained-glass windows, sculptures and painting masterpieces. The house, its priceless contents and the exquisite **gardens** *(see Parks and Gardens)* were bequeathed to a private foundation in 1970, and opened as a museum in 1975.

Erasmus House ★★
(Maison d'Érasme)

Rue du Chapître 31, Anderlecht. Metro: St-Guidon. Open Tue–Sun 10am–6pm. €1,25 (includes Anderlecht Béguinage). Reserve in advance for a guided tour in English. 02 521 13 83. erasmushouse.museum.

This historic residence, where scholar and religious reformer **Desiderius Erasmus** (1466-1536) lived during his time in Brussels in 1521, today contains five rooms filled with Gothic and Renaissance furnishings. Visitors can get a glimpse of both the intellectual and private life of Erasmus as well as admire antique books and paintings. Outside, stroll through the garden of medicinal plants that Erasmus would have used to treat himself in the 16C; and explore the philosophical garden, containing plants and flowers that Erasmus encountered on his many journeys.

Horta Museum★★
(Musée Horta)

Rue Américaine 25, St-Gilles. Trams 81, 92 or 97. Open Tue–Sun 2pm–5:30pm. Closed Mon & public holidays. €7. 02 543 04 90. www.hortamuseum.be.

Occupying two narrow houses built by architect Victor Horta (1861–1947) as his home and studio between 1898 and 1901, the Horta Museum is a masterpiece of function and elegance, and a tribute to Art Nouveau at its finest. Here, glass and iron play with curves and counter-curves to graceful and beautiful effect.

MUST SEE

Note the original mosaics and stained-glass windows, as well as the curving marble staircase – one of Horta's most beautiful creations. The architect's scale models are also on display.

Ixelles Museum

©Georges Strens 2011/Ixelles Museum

Ixelles Museum★★
(Musée d'Ixelles)

Rue J-van-Volsem 71, Ixelles. Tram 81: Flagey. Open Tue–Sun 1pm–6.30pm, Sat–Sun 10am–5pm. Closed Mon & public holidays. 02 515 64 21. www.museedixelles. irisnet.be.

Inaugurated in 1892, this small museum packs a big punch. It has an excellent collection of 18C–20C artwork, including a sketch by Albrecht Dürer, entitled *The Stork*. One of the most iconic collections of the museum is the entire production of lithographic works by Henri de Toulouse-Lautrec, as well as roughly 700 posters by Belgian and European artists, including Belle-Époque works and early advertising posters.

Constantine Meunier Museum★
(Musée Constantin Meunier)

Rue de l'Abbaye 59, Ixelles. Tram 94. Open Tue–Sun 10am–noon, 1pm–5pm. Closed Mon, holidays, and weekends in July & Aug. 02 508 32 11.

This museum occupies the former studio/house of 19C Belgian painter and sculptor **Constantine Meunier** (1831–1905), who devoted himself to depicting the world of labor and workers. More than 170 of Meunier's sculptures and 100 of his paintings now decorate the interior.

©KMSKB –MRBAB, Brussels, Belgium
Constantine Meunier Museum

Wittockiana Library★
(Bibliotheca Wittockiana)

Rue du Bémel 21, Woluwé-St-Lambert. Tram 39 or 44: Jules César. Open Tue–Sat 10am–5pm. Closed Mon & public holidays. €4. 02 770 53 33. www.wittockiana.org.

Located in the leafy commune of Woluwé-St-Pierre, this museum was created by a passionate book lover, industrialist Michael Wittock, and is the only institution of its kind in Belgium. The library contains roughly 1,100 volumes, including rare bound editions from the 16C to the 20C as well as important documents that recount the history of Belgium and Brussels.

The Anderlecht Béguinage

Rue du Chapître 8, Anderlecht. Metro: St-Guidon. Open Tue–Sun 10am–5pm. €1,25 (includes Erasmus House). 02 521 13 83.

This museum was set up in 1930 in the smallest Béguinage in Belgium, where only eight Béguine nuns lived. It consisted of two buildings, one from the 16C and the other from the 18C, built around an inner courtyard with a view of the **Collegiate Church of Saints Peter and Guy★** *(see Churches).* The museum's holdings include religious art and artifacts as well as documents that detail a thousand years of Anderlecht history.

Cantillon Brewery Museum
(Musée de la Gueuze–Brasserie Cantillona)

Rue Gheude 56, Anderlecht. Metro: Midi. Open Mon–Fri 9am–5pm, Sat 10am–5pm. Closed public holidays. €4. 02 521 49 28. www.cantillon.be.

Nothing says Brussels like Gueuze – a type of sparkling Lambic beer *(see p126)* unique to Brussels and made here from organically grown grain. This museum doubles as the operational Cantillon Brewery from October to March, when visitors can follow the brewing process through various rooms in the last remaining family brewery in Brussels, which dates back to the Middle Ages.

Clockarium

Boulevard August Reyers 163, Schaerbeek. Metro: Diamant. Guided tours Sun at 3:05pm. €6. 02 732 08 28. www.clockarium.org.

This peculiar museum sheds light on a decorative and now-forgotten craze, which was popular in Belgium and Northern France during the period between WWI and WWII. More than 1,300 earthenware clocks and chimney decorations tick away here in an Art Deco house. Don't be late – tours start at 3:05pm sharp!

Clockarium

Herge Museum

Hergé Museum
(Musée Hergé)

Rue du Labrador, 26, Louvain-la-Neuve (30km/18.5mi southeast of Brussels). Open Tue–Fri 10:30am–5:30pm, Sat–Sun 10am–6pm. Closed Mon. €9,50. 01 048 84 21. www.museeherge.com.

Southeast of Brussels, in the university town of Louvain-la-Neuve, the eagerly awaited Hergé Museum opened its doors in 2009. Here, photographs, documents and original plates catalog the life of Belgian-born artist George Remi, creator of the character Tintin, an intrepid young reporter who took the world by storm as he traveled to far-flung destinations with his dog, Snowy.

Museums of the Far East

Avenue Van Praet 44, Laeken. Tram 3 or 7: Pavillon chinois. Open Tue–Fri 9:30am–5pm, Sat–Sun 10am–5pm. Closed Mon & holidays. €4. 02 268 16 08. www.kmkg-mrah.be.

Situated in the municipality of Laeken, the collections of the Museums of the Far East are housed in the **Japanese Tower** and the **Chinese Pavilion** *(see Grand Architecture for both)*. The former displays Japanese export art, while the latter exhibits a fine collection of 18C and 19C Chinese porcelain. Nearby, the **Japanese Museum of Art** holds 12,000 works from the Edo period (1600–1868).

René Magritte Museum

Rue Esseghem 135, Jette. Metro: Belgica. Open Wed–Sun 10am– 6pm. €7. 02 428 26 26. www.magrittemuseum.be.

Want more Magritte? Don't overlook the original Magritte museum in the commune of Jette, located in the house where the artist and his wife, Georgette, lived for 24 years (1930–1954). A permanent collection here displays more than 400 original documents, revealing a biographical journey through René Magritte's life.

What's In A Name?
Tintin's creator, George Remi, wrote under the name Hergé. This nom de plume derives from Remi's initials, R.G. – which are pronounced "air jay" in French.

MUSEUMS IN GREATER BRUSSELS

CHURCHES

Travel to any European city, and you'll find that churches often form their heart. Whether you are pious or just simply curious, places of worship in Brussels are also places of wonder, and house remarkable art, spirit and history.

Abbey of Our Lady of Cambre

©Marcel Vanhulst/visitbrussels.be

Abbey of Our Lady of Cambre★★
(Abbaye Nôtre-Dame-de-la-Cambre)

Avenue Emile Duray 11, Ixelles. Tram 94: Abbaye. Open Mon–Fri 9am–noon, 3pm–6pm, Sat–Sun 3pm–6pm. 02 648 11 21.

To the south of the Ixelles Ponds, this 14C Cistercian abbey houses the École Nationale Supérieure d'Architecture et des Arts Décoratifs, the college known as "La Cambre," and the Institut Géographique National. The main semicircular **courtyard** is surrounded by abbey buildings. Note the marvelous statue of **The Mocking of Christ** by Albert Bouts in the church's nave.

Cathedral of Saints Michael and Gudula★★
(Cathédrale Sts-Michel-et-Gudule)

Place Ste-Gudule, Upper Town. Metro: Gare Centrale. Open Mon–Fri 7am–6pm, Sat 8:30am–3:30pm, Sun 2pm–6pm. 02 217 83 45.

Location of several royal weddings, the Gothic church dedicated to the archangel Michael and the

---

"Peasant" Bruegel

Flemish Renaissance painter **Pieter Bruegel the Elder** (1525–1569) was renowned for his landscape paintings, which often included scenes of peasant life. His observations of the joys and toils of everyday life emerged in works such as *Peasant Wedding* and *The Cripples* (both done in 1568). The 16C house where the painter once lived is located at Rue Haute 132, near **Church of Our Lady of the Chapel** (see p78).

MUST SEE

martyr St. Gudula – the patron saints of Brussels – is a crowd pleaser. The cathedral sits on Treurenberg Hill between Lower Town and Upper Town and was built in several stages, beginning in the 13C and ending with the two massive towers (designed by Van Ruysbroeck) in the 15C. The transept is lit by two lovely 6C **stained-glass windows★**, and carvings of Adam and Eve decorate the eye-catching Baroque pulpit.

Collegiate Church of Saints Peter and Guy★
(Collégiale des Saints-Pierre-et-Guidon)

Place de la Vaillance, Anderlecht. Metro: St-Guidon. Open Mon–Fri 9am–noon & 2pm–5pm. 02 523 02 20.

This Late Gothic collegiate church, dedicated to St. Peter and St. Guy of Anderlecht, dates from the 14C and 15C. Inside, remnants of frescoes illustrate the life of St. Guy, who died in 1012 and is buried in the Romanesque crypt. He is venerated as the patron saint of peasants and the protector of horses.

Church of Our Lady of Sablon★
(Église Nôtre-Dame-du-Sablon)

Place du Grand Sablon, Upper Town. Metro: Parc.Open Mon–Fri 9am–6:30pm, Sat, Sun 10am–7pm. Closed during services. 02 511 57 41.

This Flamboyant Gothic church, started in 1400 and completed around 1550, was the chapel of the Crossbowmen's Guild. Built

to house the Holy Sacrament, the richly decorated "sacrarium" was added to the side of the apse in 1549. The stained-glass windows in the airy chancel are illuminated from inside at night.

Church of St. Denis★
(Église St-Denis)

Rue des Abbesses 15, Forest. Tram 97: St-Denis. Tours mid-May–mid-Sept Fri–Sun 10am–noon & 3pm–5pm. 02 344 87 19. forest-saint-denis.bxl.catho.be.

The original 12C Romanesque structure was replaced in the 13C with the charming Gothic church you see today, which contains the 12C tomb of St. Alène.

National Basilica of the Sacred Heart★
(Basilique nationale du Sacré-Coeur)

Parvis de la Basilique 1, Koekelberg. Metro: Simonis. Open daily 9am–5pm. Dome access May–Oct only, €3. 02 425 88 22.

Located in an innocuous suburb of Brussels, this massive cathedral can be seen from just about any elevated location in the city center on a clear day. King Léopold II, determined to build a vast church for the burgeoning population of Brussels, ordered construction of the basilica in 1905. It was completed in 1970 and is dedicated to Belgian soldiers who never returned from war. Climb up to the 90m/295ft-high copper dome for a beathtaking view.

Chapel of Marie the Wretched
(Chapelle de Marie-la-Misérable)

Avenue de la Chapelle 37, Woluwé-St-Lambert. Metro: Roodebeek. Open daily 7:30am–6pm.

The moving story of the namesake of this 14C Brabant Gothic chapel was told by the playwright Michel de Ghelderode (interred at **Our Lady of Laeken**) in his 1952 play *Marie la Misérable*. His character, a young peasant girl known for her beauty and purity, refuses a young man's advances. The rebuffed lover slips a valuable vase into her bag, then accuses her of theft. She is unjustly condemned, and subsequently buried alive as punishment for her alleged crime.

Church of Our Lady of Laeken
(Église Nôtre-Dame-de-Laeken)

Parvis Nôtre Dame, Laeken. Metro: Bockstael. Open Tue–Sun 2pm–5pm. 02 478 20 95.

Church of Our Lady of Laeken

©Julian Love/Apa Publications

This neo-Gothic church was begun in 1854 by Joseph Poelaert, and dedicated to Louise-Marie, first queen of the Belgians and wife of Léopold I.

The **crypt** contains the royal family's tombs, including former kings Léopold II and Baudouin. Behind the church, the **cemetery** is the final resting place of such luminaries as playwright Michel de Ghelderode, the church's architect Joseph Poelaert, and violinist Charles de Bériot and his wife, opera singer Maria Malibran.

Church of Our Lady of the Chapel
(Église Nôtre-Dame-de-la-Chapelle)

Place de la Chapelle 1, Lower Town. Metro: Gare Centrale. Open Mar–Oct daily 9am–7pm, Nov–Feb daily 9am–6pm. 02 513 53 48.

In 1134 King Godefroid I built a chapel outside the city walls to serve the area's craftsmen living in nearby Les Marolles. In 1250, the church became a pilgrimage site, thanks to the donation of five pieces of Christ's Cross. A fire destroyed most of the church in 1405, and it was rebuilt in the Brabant Gothic style. Treasures inside include a memorial to 16C Belgian painter **Pieter Bruegel the Elder** (*see sidebar, p77*), who was buried in the church in 1569.

Church of St. Jacques on Coudenberg
(Église St-Jacques-sur-Coudenberg

Place Royale, Upper Town. Metro: Parc. Open Tue–Sat 1pm–6pm, Sun 8:45am–5pm. 02 511 78 36.

The last in a string of places of worship on this site, this church has changed faces and purposes several times during its long history. A chapel was first built here in the 12C to serve the dukes of Brabant. When the **Coudenberg Palace** was constructed in the 13C, the church became the ducal chapel. The fire of 1731 that destroyed the palace also leveled the chapel; the present Neoclassical church was consecrated in 1787.

Church of St. John the Baptist at the Béguinage
(Église St-Jean-Baptiste-au-Béguinage

Place du Béguinage, Lower Town. Metro: Ste-Catherine. Open year-round Tue–Sat 10am–5pm, Sun 10am–8pm. 02 217 87 42.

With its three-gabled Flemish Baroque façade, this 1676 church is considered one of the most beautiful in Belgium.
It was once the centerpiece of Brussels' largest Béguinage, a community for single pious women in the 13C *(see sidebar, above)*. The interior preserves many of its Gothic elements.

The Red Convent
(Le Rouge Cloître)

Rue de Rouge-Cloître 4, Auderghem. Tram 44: Auderghem Forêt. Garden open Mon–Fri. Interior open Tue–Thu 2pm–5pm, Sat–Sun 2pm–6pm. €3. 02 660 55 97. www.rouge-cloitre.be.

The convent lies east of Auderghem in the **Sonian Forest★★** *(see Parks and Gardens)*. The peaceful grounds include an 18C abbey, the old priory farm and a miller's house. Other buildings hold an **Art Center** and the **Sonian Forest Visitor Center**.

Royal Chapel
(Chapelle Royale)

Place du Musée 2, Upper Town. Metro: Parc. 02 213 49 40. www.eglisedumusee.be.

The Protestant community only gained legal status in Brussels In 1804, when It was given this small church (built in 1760). When Belgium gained independence in 1831, King Léopold I, a Protestant himself, worshipped here. The church is an acoustically appealing venue for chamber concerts.

CHURCHES

CHÂTEAUX AND PALACES

There are more castles, manor houses, farm castles, and citadels per square mile in Belgium than anywhere else in the world. While you're here, take some time to see a few of the places that were – and still are – fit for kings and queens.

Stoclet Palace★
(Palais Stoclet)

Avenue de Tervuren 279-281, Woluwé-St-Pierre.Tram 39 or 44: Léopold II. Closed to the public.

Austrian architect Josef Hoffmann built this magnificent residence for banker and art lover Adolphe Stoclet between 1905 and 1911. The marble-clad façade displays clean architectural lines, and four copper figures by Franz Metzner adorn the top of the house. Inside, commissioned works by **Gustav Klimt** decorate the dining room. The sketches of Klimt's work for the dining room are part of the permanent collection of the Museum of Applied Arts in Vienna. The mansion, a UNESCO World Heritage Site, is still occupied by the Stoclet family.

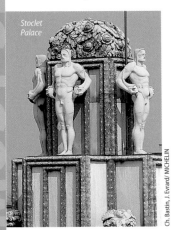

Stoclet Palace

Ch. Bastin, J. Evrard/ MICHELIN

Château de Val-Duchesse

Boulevard du Sovereign, Woluwé-St-Pierre. Tram 94: Empain. Closed to the public.

This castle is actually a former priory, named for the woman who founded it in 1262, Adelaide of Burgundy, Duchess of Brabant and widow of Henry III (the Duke of Brabant). The present-day château was built as a residence for the prioress in 1780. Now owned by the Belgian Royal Trust, the former priory is probably best known for its role in 20C history.

In 1956, the foreign ministers of the six member states of the European Coal and Steel Community (ECSC) met at the château for the Intergovernmental Conference on the Common Market and Euratom. This meeting led to the Treaties of Rome in 1957, the foundation of the European Economic Community.

Château Malou

Avenue Jean-François Debecker 3, Woluwé-St-Lambert. Metro: Roodebeek.

Built in 1776 by a wealthy merchant named Lambert de Lamberts, this Neoclassical château changed hands several times. After Belgium gained its independence from the United Kingdom of the Netherlands, the manor eventually passed on to the finance minister

Egmont Palace

©ARCO J De Meester/age fotostock

of the new Belgian government, **Jules Malou** (1810–1886). Malou occupied the building from 1853 onward, and the building has retained his name ever since. The municipality of Woluwé-St-Lambert, a quiet neighborhood of Brussels, now owns the château. The building is primarily used for cultural activities and exhibitions. The surrounding 8ha/20-acre **Parc Malou** is the largest park in Woluwé-St-Lambert, as well as the oldest. In the park, visitors will encounter an old gristmill, a playground for children, shady paths along the Woluwé River, and a pond frequented by ducks and swans.

Egmont Palace
(Palais d'Egmont)

Petit Sablon 8, Upper Town. Tram 92: Petit Sablon. Closed to the public.

Françoise of Luxembourg and her son, Lamora, Count of Egmont, built the 16C mansion located just behind the **Place du Petit Sablon★** between 1548 and 1560. The property passed on to the family of the Princes of Arenberg,

who was forced to sell it to the city of Brussels after World War I. Today the Belgian Ministry of Foreign Affairs uses the palace for receptions. Adjacent **Egmont Park** *(see Parks and Gardens)* is an ideal place for a stroll.

Palace of Charles of Lorraine
(Palais de Charles de Lorraine)

Place du Musée 1, Upper Town. Metro: Parc. Open Wed & Sat 1pm–5pm. Closed Sun–Tue, Thu, public holidays & last week of Dec. €3. 02 519 53 11. See Museums.

This palace holds the Neoclassical-style apartments of Charles of

---

Crowning the King

Although Belgium was recognized as an independent country in 1830, the monarchy was not established until 1831. On July 21 of that year, Léopold I, prince of Saxe-Coburg and Gotha, took the constitutional oath, becoming the first king of the Belgians. July 21 is Belgium's **National Day**, celebrated with great fanfare around the country.

Lorraine, Governor General of the Austrian Netherlands (1744–1780). Charles was said to have been a great patron of the arts, and it is rumored that a young Mozart once played for him here.

Palace of Coudenberg
(Palais de Coudenberg)

Place des Palais 7, Upper Town.
Enter through the BELvue Museum.
Metro: Parc. Open Tue–Fri 10am–
5pm, Sat–Sun 10am–6pm. 02 512
28 21. www.coudenberg.com.

Now a major archeological site underneath the **Place Royale★** (and connected to the **BELvue Museum**; *See Museums*), the Palace of Coudenberg presided over Brussels beginning in the 12C. Called the Palace of Brussels then, this residence of Charles V was considered one of the most beautiful palaces in Europe. After a fire destroyed it in 1731, and Place Royale was built over the ruins in the 1770s, the Palace of Coudenberg was all but forgotten. In 1910, archaeological digs unearthedthe old city wall and the

ducal palace. When work began on the foundations of the palace chapel in 1986, no one could have guessed what new secrets would be uncovered. Major excavations took place in the 1990s, and as of 2000, the public can visit the underground palace and its main buildings, along with the Rue d'Isabelle, a route used by the Archduchess Isabelle on her way to Mass in the cathedral.

Royal Castle of Laeken
(Château Royal de Laeken)

Avenue du Parc Royal. Laeken.
Metro: Stuyvenbergh.
Closed to the public.

The Royal Castle of Laeken has been the main residence of the Belgian royal family since 1831, when King Léopold II took the throne. It lies just outside of the center of Brussels in the area known as Laeken, surrounded by a beautiful park that contains other notable landmarks (the **Atomium★**, the **Japanese Tower**, the **Chinese Pavilion** and the stunning **Royal**

Cellars of the main building, Palace of Coudenberg

Hotel With a View

In 1776, a wine merchant named Philippe De Proft was authorized by Empress Maria-Theresa to build a hotel next to the Royal Palace that would be suitable for wealthy travelers. The private establishment was named **Hôtel de Belle-Vue**, after the street that ran along Brussels Park, now called Place des Palais. Among the first distinguished guests here were French nobles, including several members of the royal family, who fled to Brussels after the 1789 revolution. Napoleon is said to have dined at the hotel, and the Duke of Wellington purportedly met here with his general staff a few days before the battle of Waterloo – though probably not on the same night as the French emperor. The hotel now houses the **BELvue Museum★** *(see Museums).*

Greenhouses of Laeken★★; *see Grand Architecture).*

The palace was constructed as a summer retreat for Dutch and Austrian nobility between 1782 and 1784 and was designed by French architect Charles de Wailly. Partly destroyed by fire in 1890, the castle was rebuilt by Alphonse Balat, who also designed the Royal Greenhouses. French architect Charles Girault gave the château its present face in 1902. Upon their accession to the throne in 1993, King Albert II and Queen Paola preferred to remain living at **Belvédère Castle**, another château on the park grounds. Famous guests at the Royal Castle of Laeken include Napoleon Bonaparte, who stayed at the château with Empress Josephine in August 1804. The current occupants are the Duke and Duchess of Brabant.

Royal Palace
(Palais Royal)

Place des Palais, Upper Town. Metro: Parc. Open late Jul–Sept, Tue–Sun 10:30am–5:30pm. www.monarchie.be.

Standing opposite the Belgian Parliament, on the other side of the Royal Park, the Royal Palace is where His Majesty the King receives dignitaries and exercises his official duties as the head of state. Construction of the modern palace began in the 1820s on the site of the **Palace of Coudenberg**, and work continued under King Léopold II.

Each year after the July 21 National Day celebration, the palace opens to the public and visitors are able to tour several rooms, including the **Throne Room** and the **Hall of Mirrors**, whose ceiling shimmers with the blue-green carapaces of more than a million Thai Jewel Beetles. Artist Jan Fabre and a team of 29 people spent three months completing this painstaking task.

Visits also include the **Small White Room**, which was a wedding present from King Louis-Philippe of France to King Léopold I, who married Louis-Philippe's daughter, Louise-Marie.

Kitty-corner to the Royal Palace, the **Palais des Académies** was the residence of the Prince of Orange. The building is currently used to host events for the Royal Academy of Sciences and other organizations.

CHÂTEAUX AND PALACES

PARKS AND GARDENS

Despite it being an urban epicenter bustling with more than a million people, Brussels prides itself on being one of the greenest capitals in Europe. With more than 8,000 hectares (almost 20,000 acres) of parks, forests, grassy patches and hidden gardens, there is always an unexpected place to plant yourself. When the sun is out, Belgians love to sprawl out on these gorgeous greens.

David and Alice van Buuren Museum★★

Avenue Leo Errera 41, Uccle. Tram 3, 23 or 24: Churchill. Open year-round Wed–Mon 2pm–5:30pm. Closed Tue. €10. 02 343 48 51. www.museumvanbuuren.com. See Museums.

This museum, filled with decorative arts and artwork collected by Alice and David van Buuren, displays another masterpiece outside. Spread over four acres, the enchanting **garden** complements the Art Deco styling of the house and draws visitors year-round. It may be out of the way, but it's worth the trek to find your way through the Labyrinth, to see the

adorable heart-shaped hedges in the Heart Garden, and stroll in the fragrant Rose Garden.

🌲 Sonian Forest★★
(Le Forêt de Soignes)

59km/37mi southeast of Brussels.

South of the Bois de la Cambre, this beech forest stretches over 10,000 acres (almost to Waterloo) and is best explored via its miles of foot trails and bike paths. Any time of year is worth a visit, but fall, when the colors are changing, is particularly vibrant. Within the verdant surrounds are treasures to be discovered, among them the **Arboretum of Tervuren★** *(see Excursions)*, the **Red Convent**, and the remains of an Augustinian abbey in the hamlet of **Groenendael**, founded by spiritual writer and mystic Jan van Ruysbroeck.

🌲 Brussels Park★
(Parc de Bruxelles)

Rue Royale at Place des Palais, Upper Town. Metro: Parc.

Also known as Parc Royale (Royal Park), this green space across the street from the Royal Palace is a symmetrical gem, popular in the summer when the trees and manicured shrubs are in full bloom. The land, once the hunting ground of the dukes of Brabant, was laid

Garden of David and Alice van Buuren Museum

©Michel de Bray/Musée van Buuren

out with formal gardens in the 18C. The entire area of the Royal Park and the Place Royale is situated on the site where the medieval court of Brabant reigned from the enormous **Palace of Coudenberg**, dating from the 11C *(see Châteaux and Palaces)*. The **Théâtre Royal du Parc** *(see Performing Arts)* is located also in the park.

Cambre Woods★
(Bois de la Cambre)

Avenue Louise at Avenue Lloyd George, Ixelles. Tram 3 or 23: Cambre-Étoile.

Located at the top of chic Avenue Louise, this vast wooded park is actually the northernmost part of the Sonian Forest and has loads of open space, pathways, play areas and a small lake. In the center of the lake, Robinson Island holds the **Chalet Robinson** *(see Must Eat)*, a Brussels institution and a fantastic restaurant. The park is a year-round favorite for ice-skating, horseback riding, biking, canoeing, fishing or simply relaxing – especially on Sundays when the park's roads are closed to traffic.

🌿 Cinquantenaire Park
(Parc du Cinquantenaire)

Between Avenue Tervuren and Rue de la Loi, Upper Town. Metro: Schuman or Mérode.

Planned by King Léopold II in the late 19C, this park (also called Jubilee Park), boasts one of Brussels' most visible monuments: the **Triumphal Arch** *(see Grand Architecture)* built to celebrate Belgium's 50th year of independence. The pretty park edging the monumental buildings

Go Green
September 22 is **World Car-Free Day**, and in Brussels, thousands take to their bikes and public transportation to get around the city. The event is held on the nearest Sunday to the "official" date and is a great chance to go green and explore the numerous green patches of Brussels, without the hassle of traffic.

is ideal for walking and running. It is also the site of military parades and a summer drive-in movie; it's also the starting point of the **Brussels Marathon** *(see Calendar of Events)*.

Egmont Park
(Le Parc d'Egmont)

Between Boulevard de Waterloo and the Place du Petit Sablon, Upper Town. Metro: Louise.

Located near the uninspiring Hilton Hotel on Boulevard de Waterloo, a cobbled lane leads to a forgotten patch of green called Egmont Park, named for the palace built there between 1548 and 1560 for Françoise of Luxembourg and her son, Lamoral, the Count of Egmont. The restored Orangerie is now a coveted lunch table, and a bronze statue of Peter Pan, among other delights, adorns this urban oasis.

Ixelles Ponds
(Les Étangs Ixelles)

Avenue de l'Hippodrome, Upper Town. Tram 81: Flagey.

Two elongated ponds surrounded by mature trees and stylish Art Deco and Art Nouveau homes

PARKS AND GARDENS

Photo Op

The stairs above the formal park *(between the Musical Instrument Museum and Lower Town)* in the **Mont des Arts** area are a popular spot for photographs, with the picturesque spire of the **Hôtel de Ville** *(see Grand Architecture)* as a backdrop.

make this one of Brussels' most desirable areas. The ponds are fed by the Maelbeek River, and are an extension of the nearby gardens of the **Church of Our Lady of Cambre★★**. Every weekend, a market *(Fri–Sun 7am–1pm)* sprawls out alongside the ponds.

Laeken Park
(Parc de Laeken)

Avenue du Parc Royal, Laeken. Metro: Stuyvenbergh.

The wide-open spaces that surround the Château of Laeken, the home of the Belgian royal family, might seem a bit sterile, but there is much to see here. Start with the gothic **Monument of the Dynasty**, erected in honor of King Léopold I. From certain vantage points there are views over Brussels. The spectacular **Royal Greenhouses★★**, the **Japanese Tower** and the **Chinese Pavilion** *(see Grand Architecture for all three)*, will also catch your eye.

Le Botanique

Rue Royale 236, St-Josse. Metro: Botanique. Open year-round daily 10am–6pm. 02 218 37 32. www.botanique.be.

Though it's no longer the Botanical Gardens of Brussels, this19C greenhouse and surrounding sculpture garden makes for a quiet picnic spot in a bustling corner of the city. More than 50 statues were added here between 1894 and 1898, an endeavor overseen by sculptors Charles van der Stappen and Constantin Meunier. "Le Bota," as it's known, is now a

Leopold Park

©Olivier van de Kerchove/visitbrussels.be

Garden Squares

Rue Archimède, European Quarter. Metro: Schuman. Delightful **Place Ambiorix** and **Place Marie-Louise** will enchant lovers of formal gardens and fans of Art Nouveau architecture alike. The houses surrounding Place Ambiorix in Upper Town represent the work of several well-known architects, including **Victor Horta**. The name of the square is a tribute to the Belgian national hero, the Gaul, Ambiorix, who fought against the forces of Julius Caesar. Connected to Ambiorix square via Avenue Palmerston, Place Marie-Louise has a large lake surrounded by a little park full of fountains, and flowers in the spring.

popular cultural center whose calendar includes a diverse schedule of performances *(see Performing Arts)*.

Leopold Park
(Parc Léopold)

Rue Belliard 133, Upper Town. Metro: Schuman.

The sense of peace found in this park contrasts starkly with the austere buildings of the European Quarter. The postage-stamp-sized patch of green has a few interesting sites, like **Eggevoort Tower**, the remains of a medieval domain; and the **Solvay Library**, a jewel of Brussels architecture *(not open to the public)*. The park also has a play area and a pond where you can feed the ducks.

🚣 Mellaerts Ponds
(Les Étangs Mellaerts)

Avenue de Tervuren, corner of Blvd. du Souverain, Woluwé-St-Pierre. Tram 39 or 94: De Villalobar.

Just down the road from Woluwé Park is a small yet pleasant spot that's ideal for a family outing. Here, you can rent a paddleboat, feed the swans, have an ice-cream cone (in summer), or battle it out on the mini-golf greens.

The Red Convent
(Le Rouge Clôitre)

Rue de Rouge-Clôitre 4, Auderghem. Tram 44: Auderghem Forêt or Garen. Garden open Mon–Fri. 02 660 55 97. www.rouge cloitre.be. See Churches.

Located on the edge of the **Sonian Forest★★**, this former abbey is a popular starting point for forest walks, and is also a great destination by itself. Check out the surrounding ponds and the Jean Massart Garden, containing some 400 medicinal plants and fruit trees. It was established in 1922 by its namesake, the renowned Belgian botanist.

Woluwé Park
(Parc de la Woluwé)

Avenue de Tervuren, Woluwé-St-Lambert. Tram 39 or 44: Chien Vert.

This 71ha/175-acre park lies between the leafy neighborhoods of Woluwé-St-Pierre and Woluwé-St-Lambert and offers visitors a soothing place to walk, play, or bike. There are three lakes and enough open space for kids to play ball or throw a Frisbee. When snow falls, Woluwé Park is popular with the sledding set.

PARKS AND GARDENS

EXCURSIONS

**One of the best things about Brussels is its position in the heart of
Europe, making it an easy base from which to satisfy your wanderlust.
Aside from Paris, Amsterdam and London, all being a mere two-hour
train ride away, Antwerp★★★, Bruges★★★, Ghent★★★ and more
sights worth a detour all lie within easy reach of the capital.**

ANTWERP★★★

*The route marked on the map
offers a tour of the city's highlights.*

Called "The Metropolis" by locals,
Antwerp *(56km/35mi north of
Brussels)* is everything a city should
be: cultured; fashionable; and a
multifaceted patchwork of lively
neighborhoods harboring gracious
houses, grand squares, and world-
class restaurants and museums.
Yet at its heart, Antwerp is still the
proud Flemish town it has been
since it was first settled in the 3C.
Stretching along the Scheldt River,
Antwerp's historic heart, the **Old
Center★★★**, is a maze of attractive
squares, narrow streets, and
quaint passageways.

Museums
Museum Plantin-Moretus★★★
*Vrijdagmarkt 22. Open year-round
Tue–Sun 10am–5pm. Closed Mon
& major holidays. 03 221 14 50.*

www.plantin-moretus.be.
This museum occupies 34 rooms
in the house and printing works
built by printer **Christoffel Plantin**
(1520–1589). Enlarged in the 17C
and 18C by Plantin's descendents,
the Moretus family, the site
provides a fascinating history
of book production in 16C and
17C Netherlands through gilded
leatherwork, paintings, libraries,
engravings and manuscripts. The
famous *Biblia Polyglotta* (Bible in
five languages) is exhibited here,
along with the **Gutenberg Bible**,
one of only 13 left in the world.

**Royal Museum of Fine Art★★★
(Koninklijk Museum voor
Schone Kunsten)**
*Leopold de Waelplaats, 1–9.
The Royal Museum of Fine Arts
Antwerp is closed for renovation
until the end of 2017.
Check website for updates.
03 238 78 09. www.kmska.be.*

Museum Plantin-Moretus

©Antwerpen Toerisme & Congres

Designed as a temple of art, the Royal Museum of Fine Art is housed in a 19C Neoclassical building fronted by Corinthian columns crowned with bronze chariots. The four allegorical figures symbolize the arts: architecture, painting, sculpture and engraving. The collection gives an overview of the evolution of European painting from 1300 to the present and includes a treasure trove of important works, some of which will be exhibited elsewhere in Antwerp during the museum's renovation.

ModeMuseum

©Artwerpen Toerisme & Congres

Ethnographic Museum (Etnografisch Museum)★★
Suikerrui 19. Open year-round Tue–Sun 10am–5pm. Closed Mon & major holidays. €4 (free the last Wed of each month). 03 220 86 00. Ethnografischmuseum.be.
Organized thematically, this collection of some 33,000 objects documents non-European ethnic groups from Africa to the Americas. Highlights include African masks, feather costumes from South America, pre-Columbian textiles and stoneware, and ceramics from the Far East, among a host of other items.

ModeMuseum★★
Nationalestraat 28. Open Tue–Sun 10am–6pm. €7. 03 470 27 70. www.momu.be.
In a neighborhood made stylish by the younger generation of Belgian fashion designers, this *à la mode* fashion museum occupies the 19C ModeNatie building. Material from the permanent collection is displayed in rotation and arranged thematically, while the evolution of fashion is shown chronologically.

The building also houses the fashion department of the **Royal Academy of Fine Arts**, the provenance for many of Belgium's cutting-edge designers.

Museum Mayer van den Bergh★★
Lange Gasthuisstraat 19. Open Tue–Sun 10am–5pm (last admission 4:30pm).Closed Mon. €3. 03 232 42 37. museum. antwerpen.be/mayervandenbergh.
Located in an early-20C neo-Gothic house, this museum presents a remarkable group of works of art, brought together by collector **Fritz Mayer van den Bergh** (1858-1901), a connoisseur of medieval sculpture, illuminated manuscripts, tapestries and paintings. The painting entitled *Mad Meg (De Dulle Griet)* by **Bruegel the Elder** is housed here.

Rubens' House★★ (Rubenshuis)
Wapper 9–11. Open Tue–Sun 10am–5pm. Closed Mon & major holidays. €8. 03 201 15 55. museum.antwerpen.be/ rubenshuis.

Antwerp's Painter

Peter Paul Rubens was born near Cologne on June 28, 1577, where his father, an alderman of Antwerp, had been forced to take refuge when he was suspected of heresy. Rubens first saw Antwerp in ruins, at age 12, after his father's death. After spending time in Italy, he returned to Antwerp in 1608. A flood of commissions led him to set up a studio there. His students and assistants included now-prestigious names like **Jan Bruegel**, and the three Antwerp painters **Jordaens**, **Van Dyck** and **Snyders**. Rubens died in Antwerp in 1640 and was buried in **St-Jacobskerk** (St. James' Church; *Lange Nieuwstraat 73*).

The presence of artist **Peter Paul Rubens** (1577–1640) is felt everywhere in Antwerp, but most strongly in the grand house he purchased in 1610 and turned into a palace and studio, where he painted most of his works. His wife, Isabella Brant, died after bearing Rubens' three children; four years later he married Hélène Fourment. They had five more children, who were brought up here.

Butcher's Hall★★ (Vleeshuis)

Vleeshouwersstraat 38–40. Open Tue–Sun 10am–5pm. Closed Mon & major holidays. €5. 03 292 61 00. museum.antwerpen.be/vleeshuis.
A musical journey back in time awaits at the Gothic Butcher's Hall (1504) in the old harbor district. The great hall, crowned by diagonal rib vaulting, holds the Sound of the City exhibit, which includes a wonderful collection of **musical instruments★**.

Maritime Museum★★ (Nationaal Scheepvaartmuseum)

Steenplein 1. Open Tue–Sun 10am–5pm. Closed Mon. €4. 03 201 93 40.
The Maritime Museum is in the **Steen**, the fortress built after the 843 Treaty of Verdun established the new frontier. Enlarged by Emperor Charles V around 1520, the castle was restored in the 19C and 20C. Exhibits trace maritime life, with particular reference to

Rockox House

©Antwerpen Toerisme & Congres

MUST SEE

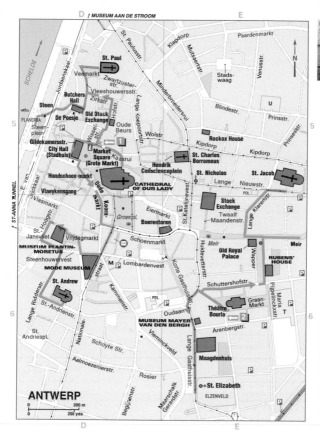

ANTWERP

Belgium, from its beginnings to the present day, through pictures, models, instruments, sculptures and documents.

Rockox House★
(Rockoxhuis)
Keizerstraat, 12. Open Tue–Sun 10am–5pm. Closed Mon. €2,50 (free the last Wed of each month). 03 201 92 50. www.rockoxhuis.be.
Nikolas Rockox (1560–1640), humanist, burgomaster of Antwerp and a friend of Rubens, was an enthusiastic collector

of objets d'art, which filled his elegant 17C home. The house is now filled with magnificent furniture, ceramics and paintings, including works by **Metsys**, **Van Dyck**, **Rubens**, and Antwerp painters **Frans Snyders** and **Joachim Beuckelaer**.

Museum Aan de Stroom (MAS)
Hanzestedenplaats 1. Open Tue–Fri 10am–5pm, Sat–Sun 10m–6pm. Temporary exhibits €8; permanent €5; combination tickets €10. 03 338 44 34. www.mas.be.

EXCURSION – ANTWERP

Cathedral of Our Lady

©Antwerpen Toerisme & Congres

MAS Boulevard

*Open Apr–Nov Tue–Sun
9:30am–10pm; Nov–Mar
9:30am–8pm. Closed Mon.*
For a free 360-degree panorama
of Antwerp, take the escalator
that rises up from the ground
floor to the 9th floor of MAS.
Once you reach the roof, the
city, the port and the river all
spread out before you in one
glorious sweep.

Between Antwerp's oldest docks,
the Bonaparte dock and the Willem
dock, the newest building on the
Antwerp skyline is the city's new
municipal museum.
From a distance, this curious
building looks like a giant Jenga
puzzle, but the architecture recalls
the 16C storehouses typical of
Antwerp's port. A large part of the
diverse collection limns Antwerp's
history from its Golden Age in the
16C to the city's position today
as Belgium's nucleus of hip.
Paving the square in front of
the MAS is a 1,600m²/17,222sq
ft mosaic by local artist **Luc
Tuymans**.

Historic Sites
Cathedral of Our Lady★★
(Onze Lieve Vrouwekathedraal)
*Gorenplaats 21. Open Mon–Fri
10am–5pm, Sat 10am–3pm,
Sun 1pm–4pm. €5. 03 213 99 51.
www.dekathedraal.be.*
The pride of Antwerp, this
imposing cathedral is the largest
in Belgium, covering 1ha/2.5
acres. Although it took from 1352
to 1521 to complete, it presents
a remarkable harmony of style.
Recent restoration has exposed
traces of the original Romanesque
church, as well as some Gothic
cellars and 15C and 16C murals. A
miracle of delicate ornamentation,
the cathedral's **tower★★★** soars
to a height of 123m/403ft. It took
a century to build and houses a
carillon of 47 bells.

Church of St. Charles
Borromeus★ (St-Carolus
Borromeuskerke)
*Hendrik Conscienceplein 6. Open
Mon–Fri 10am–12:30pm & 2pm–
5pm, Sat 10am–6pm. 03 231 37 51.*
The beautiful Baroque façade of this
"Jesuit-style" church (1621) is divided
into three sections horizontally,
with a central medallion based on

a drawing by Rubens. Inside, the barrel-vaulted brightly lit church is still striking, despite a fire in 1718, which destroyed most of the original building.

Market Square★
(Grote Markt)
Antwerp's gorgeous main square is surrounded by 16C and 17C **guildhalls**. Crowned with crow-stepped gables and delicate pinnacles, the façades of the guildhalls consist almost entirely of windows. The 1564 **Stadhuis** (Town Hall), bordering the square, displays elements of Flemish and Italian Renaissance styles. The interior was completely remodeled in the 19C.

Family Fun
Antwerp Zoo★★
(Dierentuin)
Koningin Astridplein 26 (next to the central train station). Open daily at 10am; closing times vary seasonally. € 21 adults; €17 children ages 3-17. 03 202 45 40. www.zooantwerpen.be.
This 10ha/25-acre zoological park was founded in 1843, and is one of the oldest in the world. More than 5,000 animals here encompass rare species such as white rhinos and okapis. The zoo has earned an international reputation for its participation in international breeding programs for endangered species.

Shopping
Diamonds
An estimated three-quarters of the world's uncut diamonds find their way to Antwerp, and the diamond district – which encompasses **Pelikanstraat**, **Appelmansstraat** and **Vestingstraat** around the main

train station – is home to numerous jewelers. For a list of members' shops, contact the **Antwerp Diamond Jewelers Association** (*03 227 38 91; www.adja.be*).

Fashion
Antwerp's ascent onto the international catwalks is in part due to the **Antwerp Six**, a group of young design students who took the London fashion world by storm in the 1980s *(see sidebar, p122)*. Dirk Van Saene and Walter Van Beirendonck opened **Walter** *(St. Antoniusstraat 12)* in Antwerp, and Ann Demeulemeester has a boutique on Leopold de Waelplaats. Dries van Noten has a store in **Modepaleis** *(Nationalestraat 16)*.
The broad, traffic-free **Meir** is the main shopping street of Antwerp, where you'll find large international chains tucked inside splendid 19C and 20C façades. The **Huidevetterstraat** and adjoining streets like **Wiegstraat**, the **Groendalstraat** and the **Korte Gasthuisstraat** have been taken over by fashionable stores and cafés. Smart boutiques can also be found along **Huidevetterstraat**, **Schutterhofstraat** and **Leopoldstraat**.

Little Antwerp Hands
Antwerpse handjes (Little Antwerp Hands) are the city's specialty. Made in both chocolate and cookie forms, the edible hands derive from the legend of a giant, Druoon Antigoon, who lived on the banks of the Scheldt River. It is said he extracted a toll from passersby, cutting off a hand of anyone who refused.

BRUGES★★★

In moonlight or sunlight, Bruges *(87.8km/54.6mi northwest of Brussels)* is a vision of the Middle Ages, with its peaceful canals flanked by gabled houses and stone bridges. In summer, the charms of this city in western Belgium always draw a crowd. The town's unique character, visible in the **Historic Center★★★** and along the **canals**, was recognized by UNESCO in 2000, when it was placed on the World Heritage List.

Museums

Groeninge Museum★★★
Dijver 12. Open Tue–Sun 9.30am–5pm. €8. 05 044 87 11. www.brugge.be.
This diminutive museum holds one of the greatest art collections in Northern Europe, spanning the 15C up to present day, with special attention to the outstanding collections of the **Flemish Primitives**. **Jan van Eyck** and **Hans Memling** are among the many other Flemish masters represented in the galleries here.

Memling in St. John – Hospital Museum★★★ (Memling in Sint-Jan Hospitaalmuseum)
Mariastraat 38. Open Tue–Sun 9:30am–5pm. €8 (includes admission to Onze-Lieve-Vrouw ter Potterie). 05 044 87 11. www.brugge.be.
Hans Memling was one of the leading Flemish artists of the 15C, and Sint-Janhospitaal was one of his greatest patrons.
Exhibits relate the history of the hospital, and a smaller section in the old hospital chapel is dedicated to Memling's paintings. In the **Shrine of St. Ursula**, probably the most famous of Memling's works, the reliquary depicts the life and martyrdom of St. Ursula and the 11,000 virgins who were her companions.

Arentshuis★
Dijver 16. Open Tue–Sun 9:30am–5pm. €2,50. 05 044 87 11. www.brugge.be.
In this late-18C town house, you'll find changing contemporary exhibitions and works by Bruges-born painter and engraver **Frank Brangwyn** (1867–1956).

Gruuthuse Museum★ (Bruggemuseum – Gruuthuse)
Dijver 17. Open Tue–Sun 9:30am–5pm. Closed Mon. €6. 05 044 87 11. www.brugge.be.
This Gothic building was originally where dues on the *grute* – a mixture of flowers and dried plants added to the barley or wheat used in brewing beer – were collected. The 15C residence now houses a Museum of Decorative Arts where the past lives on through Flemish objects, ranging from tapestries to a spinet made by the renowned Ruckers firm. The museum will be closed for renovations from January through March 2012.

Municipal Folklore Museum★ (Museum voor Volkskunde)
Balstraat 43. Open Tue–Sun 9:30am–5pm. Closed Mon. €3. 05 044 87 64. www.museabrugge.be.
Set in whitewashed 17C alms-houses built by the cobbler's guild, the museum showcases the folklore and traditions of western Flanders in a series of period rooms.

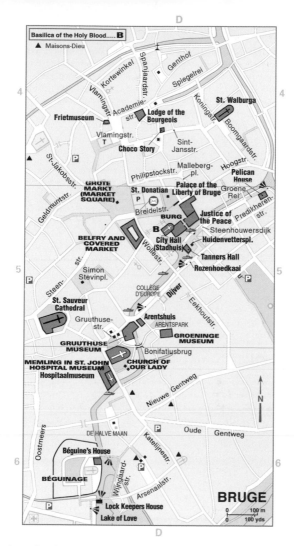

Basilica of the Holy Blood..... **B**

▲ Maisons-Dieu

Kortewinkel
Spanjaardstr.
Genthof
Spiegelrei
Vlamingstr.
Academie-str.
Frietmuseum
Lodge of the Bourgeois
St. Walburga
Koningstr.
Boomgaardstr.
Vlamingstr. T
Choco Story
Sint-Jansstr.
St-Jakobsstr.
Malleberg-pl.
Hoogstr.
Philipstockstr.
Pelican House
GROTE MARKT (MARKET SQUARE)
St. Donatian
Palace of the Liberty of Bruge
Groene Rei
Geldmuntstr.
P
Breidelstr.
BURG
Predikheren-str.
Justice of the Peace
BELFRY AND COVERED MARKET
B
City Hall (Stadhuis)
Steenhouwersdijk
Huidenvetterspl.
Wollestr.
Tanners Hall
Simon Stevinpl.
Rozenhoedkaai
P
Steen-str.
COLLÈGE D'EUROPE
Dijver
Eekhoutstr.
P
St. Sauveur Cathedral
Gruuthuse-str.
Arentshuis
ARENTSPARK
GROENINGE MUSEUM
GRUUTHUSE MUSEUM
Bonifatiusbrug
MEMLING IN ST. JOHN HOSPITAL MUSEUM
Hospitaalmuseum
CHURCH OF OUR LADY
Nieuwe Gentweg
N
Oostmeers
DE HALVE MAAN
P
Oude Gentweg
Béguine's House
Katelijnestr.
Wijngaard-str.
BÉGUINAGE
P
Arsenaalstr.
BRUGE
P
0   100 m
0   100 yds
Lock Keepers House
Lake of Love

Historic Sites

Belfry and Covered Market★★★ (Belfort and Hallen)

Markt 7. Open daily 9:30am–5pm. €8. 05 044 87 11.

These two buildings form a lovely arrangement in weathered brick. A symbol of Bruges, the 13C belfry is the largest in Belgium. The **carillon** has 47 bells that chime every quarter hour. If you're up to the challenge, climb the 366 steps up to the belfry. You'll be rewarded with a remarkable **view★★** over Bruges

Lace

Since the 1500s, many lace-making techniques have been developed, most of them in Belgium. Two main techniques are still practiced. Needle lace (a.k.a. Brussels Lace) is made in the Aalst region, while Bobbin lace is a specialty of Bruges. The latter is so expensive to make that it is no longer manufactured for commercial purposes. Drop by the **Lace Center (Kantcentrum)** for tatting demonstrations (*Peperstraat 3A; Mon–Fri 10am–12pm & 2pm–6pm, Sat 10am–5pm; €2,50; 05 045 48 45; www.kantcentrum.com*).

and the surrounding countryside. The **covered market** (*hallen* in Flemish) was constructed at the same time as the belfry and enlarged later. The market's four sections enclose a courtyard.

Begijnhof★★
Rodestraat 39. Hours vary seasonally. €2. 05 044 46 46.
The "Béguine Convent of the Vine" was founded in 1245 by Margaret, Countess of Flanders. Through an entrance near the canal is a green lawn surrounded by a 17C brick church and the white houses where the Béguines once lived (now occupied by Benedictine nuns). The **Begijnhuisje** is open to the public.

Belfry, Bruges
©Jan Darther/Toerisme Brugge

Burg★★
Between Breidelstraat and Hoogstraat.
This square is named after the castle (Burg) built by Baldwin Iron Arm. Excavations have uncovered remains of the early 9C ramparts which were pulled down so the 10C **St-Donaaskerk** could be built, only to be destroyed by the French in 1799. Four of Bruges' main buildings occupy the square: the **Basilica of the Holy Blood★**, the Gothic Town Hall (Stadhuis), the Renaissance court record office, and the old law courts.

Grote Markt★★
At the intersection of Steenstraat and Wollestraat.
A good place to start your tour in Bruges is the spacious central market place, flanked by 13C houses with crow-stepped gables, guildhalls, and the covered market in the shadow of the magnificent 13C **Belfry★★★**.

Basilica of the Holy Blood★ (Basiliek van het Heilig Bloed)
Burg 13. Open late Mar–Sept daily 9:30am–noon & 2pm–6pm; Oct–late Mar 10am–noon & 2pm–4pm. Closed during services. €1,50. 05 033 67 92. www.holyblood.org.
This basilica houses a reliquary said to contain the Holy Blood

of Christ, brought back from the Holy Land by Thierry of Alsace, Count of Flanders, on his return from the Second Crusade. The early-12C Romanesque **lower chapel**★ has kept its massive look in the cylindrical pillars and the Romanesque bas-relief of the Baptism of Christ (1300). Europe's holiest relic, the Holy Blood is displayed Fridays in the **upper chapel**. On Holy Thursday, the relic is paraded through the streets during the **Procession of the Holy Blood**★★★ (see *Calendar of Events*).

Church of Our Lady★ (Bruggemuseum – Onze-Lieve-Vrouwekerk)

Mariastraat. Open Tue–Fri 9:30am –5pm, Sat 9:30am–4:45pm, Sun 1:30pm–5pm. Chancel admission, €2,50. 05 034 53 14.

A remarkable slender brick **tower**★★ (122m/400ft tall) marks the 13C Gothic church dedicated to Our Lady. Inside is Michelangelo's white marble **Madonna and Child**★★. Among other treasures, the **chancel** contains the mausoleums of Charles the Bold and the 1498 Gothic **tomb**★★ of his daughter, Mary of Burgundy.

Holy Cross Gate (Kruispoort)

Open May–Sept Tue–Sun 9:30am– 12:30pm & 1:30pm–5pm. Closed on the Feast of the Ascension. €2. 050 44 87 64.

One of the four remaining city gates of Bruges, the Holy Cross Gate once formed part of the town walls in the northeastern part of the city. The wall north of the gate was once dotted with

20 **windmills**. Of those, two remain: **Bonne Chieremolen** was brought here in 1911 from Olsene; the original **St-Janshuismolen** windmill dates from 1770.

Family Fun
Boat Rides

Tours depart daily 10am–6pm from five different points in the historic center. €6,90. www.bruges.be.

Yes, they are touristy, but Bruges' boat tours are among the best ways to visit this storybook city. There are several boat-departure locations in the center of the city along the canals, and each offers a standard 30-minute floating presentation of Bruges, its history, and its important buildings – in multiple languages.

Shopping

The two main shopping streets in the city center, **Steenstraat** and **Noordzandstraat**, are both easy to find because they both lead to the **Grote Markt**★★.

Both are lined with mainstream chains (H&M; Zara) as well as well as one-off boutiques like **L'Heroine**, where you'll find collections by Belgian fashion icons **Dries Van Noten** and **Ann Demeulemeester**.

An extension of the Steenstraat, **Zuidzandstraat** has high-end chains such as IKKS, Massimo Dutti, and Mer du Nord. Around the **Belfry**★★★ and market square, you'll find plenty of shops selling chocolate and lace. **Breidelstraat**, connecting the Markt to the **Burg**★★, is also lined with souvenir and lace shops. Follow **Wollestraat** from the Markt to the canal, where you can catch a boat ride.

Graslei in Ghent

©Gent Toerisme

GHENT★★★

The route marked on the map offers a tour of the city's highlights.

The spiritual citadel of Flanders, Ghent *(49.4km/30.7mi northwest of Brussels)* is a university city, the second largest Belgian port, and a hub of traditional Flemish cuisine. The city's rich history and cultural treasures emerge around every corner, but especially in the **Old Town★★★** and quayside neighborhoods. From the 15C streets of the picturesque **Patershol** quarter – which harbors some excellent restaurants – to the gabled façades and distant towers seen from the waterside **Graslei★★★** and **Korenlei** districts (around the city's old port), Ghent is an effervescent feast for the senses.

Museums
**Fine Arts Museum★★
(Museum voor Schone Kunsten)**
Citadelpark. Open Tue–Sun 10am–6pm. Closed Mon. €5. 09 240 07 00. www.mskgent.be.
This large art gallery stands on the edge of the Citadelpark with its splendid octagonal bandstand dating from 1885. The museum holds extensive collections of art from the 15C to the first half of the 20C, sculptures, tapestries, and great works from the **Old Masters**.

**Municipal Museum of Contemporary Art★★
(Stedelijk Museum voor Actuele Kunst Gent)**
Citadelpark. Open Tue–Sun, 10am–6pm. Closed Mon & holidays. €6. 09 221 17 03. www.smak.be.
Across from the Fine Arts Museum, this modern art gallery goes by its Flemish acronym: SMAK. The museum, built for the 1913 World's Fair and completely renovated in 1999, is known for its gutsy and original exhibitions of work by Belgian and international artists.

Designmuseum Gent★
Jan Breydelstraat 5. Open Tue–Sun 10am–6pm. Closed Mon. €5. 09 267 99 99. www.designmuseumgent.be.
Housed in the elegant rooms of the Coninck Mansion, fine furniture and objets d'art here fill an 18C

patrician home. Emphasis is on 20C decorative arts and design; the Art Deco and Art Nouveau collections are particularly impressive.

Folklore Museum★
(Huis van Alijn)
Kraanlei 65. Open Tue–Sat 11am–5pm, Sun 10am–5pm. Closed Mon & public holidays. €2,50. 09 269 23 50. www.huisvanalijn.be.
The city's Folklore Museum fills the cottages and the Late Gothic chapel of the 14C House of Alijn, whose delightful **inner courtyard★** is bordered by white houses with tall dormer windows. Devoted to Flemish popular arts and traditions, the museum displays remarkable reconstructions of shops, domestic interiors and craftsmen's studios, recalling life in Ghent c.1900.

Industrial Society and Textile History Museum★
(Museum voor Industriële Archeologie en Textiel)
Minnemeers 9. Open Tue–Sun 10am–6pm. Closed Mon & public holidays €5. 09 269 42 00. www.miat.gent.be.
Housed in an old cotton mill (c.1905), MIAT shows Ghent's industrial history through artifacts and documents, reconstructed interiors, and machines including a **mule-jenny** smuggled in from England.

Ghent City Museum (STAM)
Godshuizenlaan 2. Open Tue–Sun 10am–6pm. Closed Mon. €6. 09 225 11 06. www.stamgent.be.
On the site of the **Bijokesite**, a Cistercian abbey and hospital, Ghent's new city museum illuminates the "Story of Ghent"

and its rich heritage. Cultural tours and visits to the abbey can be arranged from this location. The stunning abbey buildings also host exhibitions and concerts.

Historic Sites
Belfort and Lakenhalle★★★
Sint-Pietersplein 9. Open mid-Mar–mid-Nov daily 10am–1pm & 2pm–6pm (last admission 5:30pm). €5. 09 233 99 22.
Ghent's formidable belfry (91m/298ft), topped with a gilded copper dragon, symbolizes the power of the city's guilds during the Middle Ages. It was built in the 13C and 14C and has frequently been altered and restored. Adjoining it is the 15C **Cloth Hall**, or Lakenhalle, with its carillon of 52 chimes. Inside the belfry, the room called "The Secret" once contained documents setting out the town's privileged status. Check out the view of the city from the belfry's upper platform.

Castle of the Counts★★
(Gravensteen)
Sint-Veerleplein. Open Apr–Sept daily 9am–6pm; Oct–Mar daily 9am–5pm. €8. 09 225 93 06.
Extensively restored in the early 20C, the Castle of the Counts was built in 1180 by the Count of

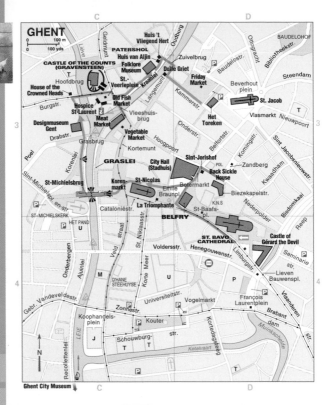

GHENT

0 ___ 100 m
0 ___ 100 yds

PATERSHOL

Huis 't Vliegend Hert

CASTLE OF THE COUNTS (GRAVENSTEEN)

Huis van Aljin Folklore Museum

House of the Crowned Heads

Hoofdbrug

St.-Veerleplein

Dulle Griet

BAUDELOHOF

Zuivelbrug

Baudelostr.

Bibliotheekstr.

Ottogracht

Oudburg

Geldmunt

Lieve

Steendam

Friday Market

Beverhout plein

St. Jacob

Burgstr.

Hospice St-Laurent

Meat Market

Old Fish Market

Vleeshuisbrug

Kraanlei

Langemunt

Kammerstr.

Het Toreken

Vlasmarkt

Nieuwpoort

Sint Jacobsnieuwstr.

Designmuseum Gent

Drabstr.

Grasbrug

Vegetable Market

Kortemunt

Hoogpoort

Onderstr.

Belfortstr.

Koningstr.

Peel

Kortenlei

GRASLEI

City Hall (Stadhuis)

Sint-Jorishof

POL.

Kwaadham

Zandberg

Sint-Michielsstr. en-str.

St-Michielsbrug

Korenmarkt

St-Nicolas

Botermarkt

Back Sickle House

Biezekapelstr.

Nederpolder

Bisdomkaai

Reep

ST-MICHIELSKERK

HET PAND

Cataloniëstr.

St. Niklaasstr.

Emile Braunpl.

La Triomphante

K.N.S St-Baafs-pl.

BELFRY

Voldersstr.

Korte Meer

Veld straat

ST. BAVO CATHEDRAL

Henegouwenstr.

Limburgstr.

Castle of Gérard the Devil

Seminarie str.

Onderbergen

Aljunlei

D'HANE STEEHUYSE

Universiteitstr.

Vogelmarkt

Lieven Bauwenspl.

Vlaanderen str.

Gebr. Vandeveldestr.

Zonnestr.

François Laurentplein

Brabantdam

Muinkschelde

Koophandelsplein

Kouter

Recolettenlei

LEIE

Schouwburg-str.

Ketelvaart

Kortedagsteeg

N

Ghent City Museum

©Gent Toerisme

St. Bavo Cathedral

Flanders, Philip of Alsace, on the site of an older keep. Inspired by Syria's Crusader castles, the ring of curtain walls adorned with watch turrets is reflected in the waters of the Leie. Highlights include the Romanesque gallery and the splendid rooms in the Count's Residence.

**St. Bavo Cathedral★★
(St-Baafskathedraal)**
*Sint-Baafsplein 4. Open Apr–Oct
Mon–Sat 8:30am–6pm, Sun
9:30am–6pm; Nov–Mar Mon–
Sat 8:30am–5pm, Sun 9:30am–
5pm. €4. 09 225 16 26.
www.sintbaafskathedraal-gent.be.*

MUST SEE

The Nose Knows

Of all Ghent's local specialties, it's a spicy mustard, **Tierenteyn-Verlent** – made here since 1790 – that embodies the quintessential flavor of this medieval city. It is believed that a member of the Tierenteyn-Verlent family, who served in the French military under Napoleon's rule, learned mustard-grinding techniques in Dijon and brought them back to Ghent. Today, the mustard is still served in stone jars with the year "1790" painted on them in blue. Inside the Tierenteyn-Verlent shop, the pungent condiment is ladled from a wooden barrel and replenished regularly from the basement factory *(Groentenmarkt 3; 09 225 83 36; www.tierenteyn-verlent.be).*

In 1540, Emperor Charles V had the church of the Abbey of St. Bavo pulled down to make way for the Spanish Palace, and the Church of St. John was renamed St. Bavo. It became a cathedral in 1561.
A few traces of the original church remain below the chancel in the massive **crypt★**.
The cathedral was built in stages, and displays elements of the Scheldt Gothic (chancel), Brabant Gothic (tower) and Late Gothic (nave) styles. Besides boasting stunning views, the **tower** on the west side of the church also serves as the entrance.
In the chapel to the left of the entrance, the **Adoration of the Mystic Lamb Altarpiece★★★** *(open Apr–Oct Mon–Sat 8:30am–5pm, Sun 1pm–5pm; Nov–Mar Mon–Sat 10:30am–4pm, Sun 1pm–4pm)* is one of Northern Europe's greatest cultural treasures. The massive polyptych by **Hubrecht** and **Jan van Eyck** was donated in 1432. Over the centuries, the altarpiece has had various owners, most of them royal. Along the way it lost several of panels, which were re-assembled in 1920 (the panel of the Righteous Judges was stolen in 1934 and replaced with a copy in 1941).

St. Nicholas Church★ (St-Niklaaskerk)
Cataloniestraat 1. Open daily 10am–5pm. 09 234 28 69.
Named for St. Nicholas, Bishop of Myra and the patron saint of merchants, this monumental parish church was built between 1200 and 1250. It is one of the best examples in Belgium of the Scheldt Gothic style.

Shopping

If you want to shop for clothing in Ghent, go to the pedestrian area bordered by **Veldstraat** and **Langemunt**, or the area around **Brabantdam**, **Magaleinstraat** and **Koestraat**.
However, the best things to shop for in Ghent are edible. Candy lovers will enjoy **Temmerman** *(Kraanlei 79; 09 224 00 41)*, Ghent's oldest sweet shop. There are *wippers* (toffees), *mokken* (anise seed-flavored biscuits), as well as *cuberdons* (raspberry-flavored sweets). For a taste of some 200 kinds of **Jenever** (gin), head to **'t Dreupelkot** *(Groentenmarkt 12; 09 224 21 20; www.dreupelkot.be).* The 15C **Groot Vleeshuis** *(Groentenmarkt 7)*, or butcher's hall, now sells specialty foods from Ghent and other regions.

OTHER EXCURSIONS

Dinant★★

65km/40mi southeast of Brussels.

This picturesque town of slate-roofed buildings enjoys a remarkable **setting★★** in the Meuse River Valley. Dominated by the massive Citadel and the onion-domed **Nôtre-Dame Collegiate Church**, Dinant is best known for its son, Adolphe Sax (sidebar, p64).

The Citadel★
N 936 Sorinnes Road. Open daily Apr–Sept 10am–6pm, Oct–Mar Sat–Thu 10am–4:30pm. €7,50. 082 22 36 70. www.citadellede dinant.be.

Perched 100m/328ft above Dinant, this fortress is accessible via cable car or a steep climb up more than 400 steps. The original 1051 fortress was rebuilt by the Bishop of Liège in 1523, destroyed by the French in 1703, and reconstructed by the Dutch in 1821. The citadel is now a museum, whose exhibits recount the history of the fortress and the town. Check out the splendid **view★★** of the town from the citadel's walls.

La Couque
Dating back to medieval times, Dinant's famous cookie is made from flour, honey and sugar and baked in carved wooden molds into a variety of intricate shapes. You may regret it if you try to bite into one of these notoriously hard biscuits. A *couque* is meant to be broken into small pieces and allowed to melt slowly in your mouth, much like a piece of caramel.

Grotte la Merveilleuse★
Rue de Philippeville 142. Visit by guided tour (50min) on the hour Jul–Aug daily 10am–6pm; Nov–Mar Sat–Sun 10am–5pm. Closed in winter. 08 222 22 10.

This cave astonishes with its colorful rock formations, which encompass a rainbow of colors including white, brown, blue and pink. The tour leads visitors along galleries on three levels; a long staircase brings you back out into the open air.

Dinant

© José Fuste Raga/age fotostock

MUST SEE

Castle of Gaasbeek

©Gaasbeek Castle

Castle of Gaasbeek★★

Kasteelstraat 40, Gaasbeek; 12km/7.5mi southwest of Brussels. Open Apr–Oct Tue–Sun, 10am–5pm. €7. 02 531 01 30. www.kasteelvangaasbeek.be.

This majestic Renaissance castle is located in Gaasbeek, a village known for its orchards as well as its local beers (Gueuze, Lambic and Kriek). One of the most magnificent castles in the area, this 13C beauty is flanked by a stunning **park★★**. Erected in 1236 for the Duke of Brabant and restored in the late 19C, the castle houses a museum containing fine decorative arts, antiquities and Belgian **tapestries** from the 15C to the 17C. The will of Flemish baroque painter **Peter-Paul Rubens** is on display in the Archives Room.

Leuven★★

28km/18mi east of Brussels.

A dynamic university town with good shopping and dining, and an effervescent nightlife, Leuven owes its fame to the **Catholic University of Leuven**, the oldest in Belgium. Leuven is also known for beer, brewed here since the 14C. The largest Belgian brewery, **Stella Artois** was launched in 1926, initially as a Christmas beer (*stella* means "star" in Latin). It was first sold in Canada and was such a commercial success that the brand became available year-round. The brew now enjoys a worldwide reputation.

Stadhuis★★★
Grote Markt 9. Visit by guided tour only daily Apr–Sept 11am & 3pm; rest of the year daily at 3pm. €2. 01 621 15 40.
Leuven's extraordinary Town Hall is an architectural masterpiece, built in the mid-15C during the reign of Philip the Good in Flamboyant Gothic style. Its vertical lines, gables, turrets and pinnacles, dormers, and almost 300 alcoves containing 19C statues are best admired from a distance. Inside are three richly decorated reception rooms.

Great Béguinage★★
(Groot Begijnhof)
Schapenstraat.
On the list of UNESCO World Heritage Sites, this convent was established in the 13C as a community for unmarried Roman Catholic women who wanted to live in a semi-monastic community without taking formal religious vows. In 1962, the Catholic University of Leuven purchased the complex – the largest Béguinage in Belgium – and restored it as accommodations for the university's students and staff.

OTHER EXCURSIONS

103

Domus

Little Domus Brewery in Leuven
(see p103) still turns out craft
brews, among them the white
beer known as Leuvense Wit/
Blanche de Louvain, and Nostra
Domus, an amber beer. Three
beers flow directly from the
brewery to the tap installed in
the on-site tavern. Group tours
are available with a reservation
(Tiensestraat 8; open Tue–Thu
& Sun 9am–1pm, Fri & Sat
9am–2pm; 01 620 14 49;
www.domusleuven.be).

St. Peter's Church★
(St-Pieterskerk)
*On Grote Markt, across from
the Stadhuis.*
St. Peter's was built in the 15C and
16C in Brabant Gothic style, on
the site of a Romanesque church.
Look inside the Gothic **interior** to
admire the pure lines, enormous
pillars and tall lancet windows.

National Botanic Garden★★
(Plantentuin)

*Nieuwelaan 38, Meise; 14km/9mi
north of Brussels. Open daily Apr–
Sept 9:30am–6:30pm, Oct–Mar
9:30am–5pm. €5. 02 260 09 20.
www.br.fgov.be.*

Located on the Bouchout
Domain in Meise, this 92ha/227-
acre garden is the largest in
Belgium, boasting more than
18,000 species of plants. Be sure
to stroll through the **Plant Palace**,
a series of 13 interconnecting
greenhouses.
Also on the domain is the **Castle
of Bouchout**, once the home of
King Léopold II's sister, Charlotte.

Ieper★ (Ypres)

103km/64mi west of Brussels.

Ieper was once one of Flanders'
great cities. Its current fame comes
from memories of World War I,
when it was the center of the Ieper
Salient, a bitterly fought-over area
protruding into German lines.
Today the town is a focal point
commemorating the victims who
died here between 1914 and 1918;
the surrounding countryside holds
some 170 military cemeteries.
Built in 1927 on the site of the old
Mennenpoort, the route taken
by soldiers marching to and
from the front line, **Menin Gate**
commemorates the more than
54,000 soldiers with no known
grave. Every evening at 8pm,
traffic stops here and buglers of
the Ieper fire brigade play a
moving tribute.

In Flanders Fields Museum★★
*Lakenhallen Grote Markt 34.
Open Apr–Nov 15 10am–6pm, mid-
Nov–Mar 31 10am–5pm. €8. 05 723
92 20. www.inflandersfields.be.*
The brutal battles of Ieper Salient
are explained here through
interactive terminals, documents,
photographs and recordings,
including the famous poem *In
Flanders Fields* by John McCrae.
The museum will be closed
from mid-November 2011 until
June 2012 while it undergoes an
extensive renovation.

Tervuren★

*12km/7.5mi east of Brussels.
Tram 44: Tervuren.*

An easy tram ride from Brussels,
Tervuren sits on the border of the
Sonian Forest★★ *(See Parks and*

Gardens) and is known for the town's lovely **Tervuren Park★** and the **Royal Museum of Central Africa★★★**, a must-see if you're in the area. The park, once highly prized for hunting, now boasts lush lawns and tranquil lakes, and paths for biking and strolling.

Royal Museum of Central Africa★★★ (Koninklijk Museum voor Midden-Afrika) *Leuvensesteenweg 13. Open year-round Tue–Fri 10am–5pm, Sat–Sun 10am–6pm. 02 769 52 11. www.africamuseum.be.*
Conceived in 1897 when King Léopold II organized an exhibition in the Colonial Palace featuring the flora, fauna, art and ethnology of the Congo, this stunning museum houses world-renowned collections of geology, zoology and cultural anthropology relating primarily to Central Africa and its colonial past. Holdings include 10,000,000 animal specimens, 180,000 ethnographic objects and 4,000 works of art, among a wealth of other artifacts. Seek out the **great gallery**, where you'll find sculptures in wood, ivory, stone and metal, plus a great collection of jewels and accessories.

Waterloo★

17.5km/11mi south of Brussels.

In Waterloo, on June 18, 1815, the Allied Anglo-Dutch forces – under the Duke of Wellington, and the Prussians, led by Field-Marshal Blucher – put an end to Napoleon's expansionist dreams and began a new chapter of European history.

The Battlefield
Route du Lion 315. Visitor Center open Apr–Oct daily 9:30am–6:30pm, Nov–Mar daily 10am–5pm. Full tour €12 (other combination tickets available). 02 385 19 12. www.waterloo1815. be/en/waterloo.
Though the geography of this famous battlefield has changed greatly since 1815 (several roads now cross it), the plain is dotted with historic buildings and commemorative monuments. A historical re-enactment with more than 2,000 participants in period costumes is held here each year on June 18 *(see Calendar of Events)*. Just outside the visitor center, the 45m/147ft-high **Butte du Lion** was built in 1826 by the Kingdom of the Netherlands on the spot where the Prince of Orange

J.D. Burton ©RMCA

Royal Museum of Central Africa

Floralia Brussels

Although the **Castle of Grand-Bigard**, or Groote-Gijgaarden *(located off the Little Ring Road, exit 11; www.grandbigard.be)*, is not open to the public, visitors flock to its vibrant gardens in spring for the annual flower show *(open early Apr–early May)*. Come wander the magnificently maintained 14ha/34.5 acres around beds bursting with tulips, daffodils, hyacinths and roses. Indoor garden fashions are presented in the newly restored greenhouse.

was wounded fighting the Imperial Guard. A cast-iron lion weighing 28 tons crowns the top of this mound, which affords a good overview of the battlefield. A 1912 rotunda holds a **panoramic painting** depicting striking episodes in the battle.

Beach at Oostende

©Toerisme Oostende

Wellington Museum

Chausée de Bruxelles 147 (N5). Open Apr–Sept 9:30am–6pm, Oct–Mar 9:30am–5pm. €5. 02 357 28 60. www.museewellington.be. Housed at the inn used as the **Duke of Wellington**'s headquarters – and where he stayed on June 17 and 18, 1815 – the museum limns the history of Waterloo.

Belgium's Beaches

www.dekust.be.

Mention Belgium, and beaches don't quickly come to mind, but the country's 65km/45mi stretch of North Sea coastline is wildly popular among Belgians. Resorts are connected via a tram, called the *Kusttram*, that runs from De Panne, near the French border, to Knokke-Heist, near the Dutch border.
Blankenberg is a small fishing port and a popular coastal resort, boasting a glass-fronted casino, wide beaches, a pier and traffic-free shopping streets. In **De Haan**, turn-of-the-century villas nestle amid 63.5ha/157 acres of woodland and sand dunes. The town is classified as one of the 15 most beautiful villages in Flanders. **Knokke-Heist** is known for its chic shops and restaurants, and some of the loveliest villas on the coast, particularly in the Het Zoute neighborhood. Nature lovers enjoy **The Zwin**, a vast nature preserve located on the border of Belgium and the Netherlands east of Knokke-Heist.
Oostende, the largest seaside resort *(110km/68mi east of Brussels)*, was a favorite of King Léopold II. It harbors a seafront promenade, a casino, and the old fishermen's district, made up of narrow streets

bounded by the beach and the harbor. To avoid traffic jams on the coast route on sunny weekends, hop on a train; the trip to Oostende takes only a little over an hour from Brussels (www.b-rail.be).

La Hulpe

20km/12.5mi southeast of Brussels.

Centerpiece of La Hulpe is the 220ha/544-acre **Domaine Solvay**, once owned by the family of industrialist Ernest Solvay, who bequeathed it to the State in 1968. The **château** overlooks a magnificent wooded **park★★** *(open summer 8am–9pm, winter 8am–6pm)*. Now an arts center, the château hosts plays and operas on its grounds *(Chaussée de Bruxelles; 111; 02 634 09 30; www. chateaudelahulpe.wallonie.be).*

Spa

140km/87mi southeast of Brussels. www.spa-info.be.

The mother of all spa towns, from which the term "spa" derives, lies in one of the loveliest parts of the Ardennes, amid the wooded rolling hills of southeastern Belgium. People from all walks of life have been coming to take the waters here since the 16C. The waters of Spa's many hot springs contain iron and bicarbonates used to treat rheumatism as well as cardiac and respiratory ailments. Today the town has loads of shops and restaurants, in addition to a well-known thermal bath.

Les Musées de la Ville d'Eaux
Avenue Reine Astrid 77B.
Open Mar–mid-Nov 2pm–6pm.
€3. 08 777 44 86. www.spavilla royale.be.
To delve into the town's history, visit these museums, which occupy part of the royal villa of Queen Maria-Henrietta, a Hapsburg princess and the second Queen of Belgium, who died in Spa in 1902. Besides exhibits about the town's baths, the museums contain a collection of **jolités**, painted wooden boxes and other objects, which are specialties of Spa.

Les Thermes de Spa
Colline d'Annette et Lubin.
Open Mon–Sat 10am–9pm, Sun 10am–8pm. €18 for 3hrs. 08 777 25 60. www.thermesdespa.com.
Established in 1868 and perched above the quaint town of Spa, the **thermal baths** are now a light-filled contemporary healing center boasting two indoor and outdoor thermal pools, a variety of treatment rooms and hammams (Turkish baths).

Spa-Francorchamps Race Circuit

Route du Circuit 38, Spa. Guided tours Mar 15–Nov 15, first and third Tue and second Wed of each month. €9,50. 08 729 37 00. www.spa-francorchamps.be. Home to the famous **Belgian Grand Prix**, which zooms into town in August, the 6.9km/4.2mi track was built in 1921. It is considered one of the most beautiful courses on the Formula 1 circuit *(see p115).*

FAMILY FUN

Brussels is a great city for kids of all ages, and thanks to a variety of indoor, outdoor, and interactive diversions, the phrase "I'm bored" will be a thing of family vacations past.

Belgian Center for Comic Strip Art★★
(Centre Belge de la Bande Dessinée)

Rue des Sables 20, Lower Town. Metro: Gare Centrale or Tram 94 to Congrès. Open Tue–Sun 10am–6pm. Closed Mon. €8 adults; €6 children ages 12-16; €3 children under 12. 02 219 19 80. www.cbbd.be. See Museums.

This museum always delivers a smile and reveals Belgium's "funny" history through comic-book characters like the intrepid young **Tintin** and the **Smurfs** – yes, they are Belgian! Three-dimensional displays, enlarged drawings, a reading room, and an on-site gift shop appeal to kids, while parents will appreciate the gorgeous setting in the Art Nouveau Waucquez Warehouses.

Manneken Pis★★

At the corner of Rue de l'Étuve and Rue du Chêne, Lower Town. Metro: Gare Centrale or Bourse. See Historic Squares.

Kids will get a giggle out of this fountain, one of Brussels' most visited and peculiar attractions. A short walk from the Grand Place, this statue of a cherubic boy relieving himself draws camera-crazy crowds who jostle to capture a photo of the bronze figure. It has become customary for visiting dignitaries to donate an outfit to the Manneken Pis, whose wardrobe counts more than 800 costumes from around the world. Check them out at the **Brussels City Museum** *(see Museums)* on the Grand Place.

Royal Belgian Institute Museum of Natural Sciences★★
(Muséum des Sciences Naturelles Institut Royal)

Rue Vautier 29, Upper Town. Metro: Maalbeek, then a 10min walk. Open Tue–Fri 9:30am–5pm; Sat–Sun 10am–6pm. Closed Mon. €7 adults; €4,50 children under 12 (free first Wed of the month after 1pm). 02 627 42 27. www.naturalscience.be.

Smurf Out Your Smurfy Side

The Smurfs (*les Schtroumpfs* in French), were created in 1958 by Belgian cartoonist Peyo, the pen name of Pierre Cullifor. The blue elfin creatures were secondary characters until 1981, when the American cartoonist duo Hanna & Barbera produced *The Smurfs* television series. Smurfs have their own language. You can speak it too: just substitute the world "smurf" for any noun, verb, adjective or adverb. "These smurfs are smurfy smurf" is way more fun to say than "these Brussels sprouts are really delicious."

Royal Belgian Institute Museum of Natural Sciences

Here, you can visit the supersized creatures called **Iguanadons** – dinosaurs that once stomped around Belgium. (Maybe that's why the country is so flat?) The well-preserved bones of 29 of these creatures were found in 1878 in the village of Bernissart, in the western part of Belgium. Ten skeletons, each measuring 10m/33ft long, have been rebuilt here, in the largest dinosaur exhibit in Europe.

In the new permanent gallery, **250 Years of Natural Sciences**, both taxidermed animals and animal skeletons tell the story of Belgium's past. Here you'll find remarkable specimens from a life-sized elephant and gorillas from the African Congo to wood from a petrified forest.

Atomium★

Boulevard du Centenaire, Atomium Square, Laeken. Metro: Heysel. Open year-round daily 10am–6pm (last admission 30min before closing). €11 adults; €8 children ages 12-18; €6 children 6-11. 02 475 47 77. www.atomium.be. See Grand Architecture.

Kids love eyeballing this odd structure, built for the 1958 World's Fair. Reaching 102m/334ft high, the nine supersized spheres represent an iron crystal enlarged 165 billion times. Inside, you'll have the sensation of being in a spaceship as internal escalators move you between the spheres. Take the kids to the uppermost sphere, where they'll have a fantastic view of Brussels.

At the foot of the Atomium, the **Bruparck** entertainment complex is where you'll find **Mini-Europe**, an IMAX theater and the **Océade** water park.

Brussels Aquarium

Avenue Émile Bossaert 27, Koekelbert. Tram 19: De Wand. Open Jun–Aug Tue–Fri 10am–6pm (noon–6pm during the school year), Sat–Sun 10am–6pm. Closed Mon. €8 adults, €5 children under 15. 02 414 02 09. www.aquariologie.be.

It's fun to spend a couple of hours here, ogling the 48 tanks that hold more than 250 small species of fish, amphibians and invertebrates.

FAMILY FUN

109

Near the **National Basilica of the Sacred Heart**★ *(see Churches)*, the public aquarium takes visitors on a watery journey from the North Sea to the Amazon River. Certain endangered species, or those that are already extinct in their natural habitat, can also be seen here.

Brussels Tram Museum

Avenue de Tervuren 364, Woluwé-St-Pierre. Tram 39 or 44: Musée du Tram. Open Apr–Oct, Sat, Sun & public holidays 1:30pm–7pm. €8 adults; €4 children. 02 515 31 10. www.mtub.be.

This former STIB depot now houses a large collection of trams, buses, taxis and a trolley, which served the capital since 1869. Many of them are still in working order. After you've admired these ancestors of modern transportation, hop aboard an old-fashioned tram and take a trip through the **Sonian Forest**★★ or to **Cinquantenaire Park** *(see Parks and Gardens for both).*

Mini-Europe

©Mini-Europe/visitbrussels.be

Mini-Europe

Avenue du Football 1, Laeken. Metro: Heysel. Open Apr–Sept, daily 9:30am–5pm; Jul–Aug Mon–Thu 9:30am–7pm; Oct–Dec Fri–Sun 9:30am–11pm. €13,40 adults; €10 children under 12. Combination tickets available with Océade. 02 474 13 13. www.minieurope.com.

If you thought it would be impossible to drag the kids on a tour of Europe, think again! All the countries in the European Union are represented here in 1:25 scale models of famous buildings and monuments. Want to take a trip to the Eiffel Tower? Why not – it's only a few steps from Big Ben. In July and August, fireworks light up the sky above Mini-Europe.

Museum of Cocoa and Chocolate
(Musée du cacao et du chocolat)

Rue de la Tête, Lower Town. Metro: Bourse or Gare Centrale. Open year-round Tue–Sun 10am–4:30pm. Closed Mon. €5.50 adults; children under 12 (with parents) free. 02 514 20 48. www.mucc.be.

Tucked into a historic house called "De Valk" (The Falcon), the name of a beer once brewed onsite, this "sweet" museum now traces chocolate through its history, from the Aztecs and Mayas to its arrival in Europe. The whole family will appreciate the praline-making demonstration given by a master *chocolatier* (pralines were invented in Belgium). Tasting is a given, and there's a shop where you can satisfy any chocolate cravings at the end of the tour.

MUST DO

Chocoholics

Belgians have had a love affair with chocolate since the 17C, when the Spaniards introduced them to the cocoa bean. Belgium's first chocolate shop, Neuhaus, opened in Brussels in 1857 and today it numbers among the country's 300 or so different chocolate companies. No vegetable shortening is used to dilute the flavor in Belgian chocolate, which is one reason for its popularity. According to the International Cocoa Organization, Belgians eat an average of 11kg/24.25lbs of chocolate a year. Who can blame them?

Océade

Avenue du Football, 1, Laeken. Metro: Heysel. Open year-round Wed–Fri 10am–6pm, Sat–Sun 10am–9pm. Closed Mon & Tue. €16,80 adults; €13,80 children between 1m15/3.5ft and 1m30/4ft. 02 478 43 20. www.oceade.be.

It's an endless summer at this water park, where the water is maintained at a comfortable 30°C/86°F all year round. Try the "Ouragan" (Hurricane) slide, reportedly the fastest in Belgium, or test out the new (in 2011) four-track family waterslide. Océade also boasts the biggest wave pool in the country as well as a host of other sprayers and splashers to spritz up the fun.

Scientastic

Boulevard Anspach 72-73, Lower Town. Metro: Bourse (access is underground in the Tram station). Open Mon–Tue & Thu–Fri 10am–5:30pm, Wed & Sat–Sun 2pm–5:30pm. €5.30. 02 732 13 36. www.scientastic.com.

Science plus fantastic equals Scientastic! This museum is the antithesis of boring, where kids can fly like a bird, make their voices

Touring Tip

Scientastic is popular with school and tour groups. Arrive at opening time to beat the rush.

sound like a duck's, take a picture of themselves in an impossible box, and experience more than 90 other hands-on attractions. Seeing, touching, smelling and feeling is all part of the fun – but don't tell the kids it's educational!

Toy Museum

Rue de L'Association 24, Upper Town. Metro: Botanique or Madou. Open year-round daily 10am–1pm & 2pm–6pm. €5; children under 4, free. 02 219 61 68. www.museedujouet.eu.

Kids can pick through the nostalgic toy box here and enjoy the displays of old rocking horses, pedal cars, antique trains, dolls and teddy bears. There's even a puppet theater onsite and games galore for children to play.

FAMILY FUN

THE GREAT OUTDOORS

Brussels' main attractions have always been its historical and cultural treasures. But sometimes you just want to blow off some steam. Luckily, in Brussels there are plenty of opportunities for outdoor – and indoor – recreation.

RECREATIONAL ACTIVITIES

Biking

In both the countryside and the cities, biking is popular in Belgium, in part because the terrain is flat, but mostly because Belgian-born professional cyclist Eddy Merckx *(see sidebar, below)* has reached Hollywood-star status in the country. Take a leisurely ride along the miles of paths that wind through the **Cambre Woods★** and the **Sonian Forest★★**, or go two-wheeling into secret corners of Brussels.

Pro Vélo
Rue de Londres 15, Ixelles. Metro: Trône. Open Mon–Fri 10am–1:30pm & 2pm–6pm, weekends 10am–noon & 12:30pm–6pm. Half-day guided tour €17. 02 502 73 55. www.provelo.org.
This growing cycling company offers a buffet of thematic guided biking tours. From Art Nouveau to Brussels for Beginners and Brussels by Night, each tour gives a new perspective on the city.

Villo!
www.villo.be.
You can't miss the Villo! bike stations – they are all over Brussels. Set up to encourage bike use in the city, this bike-sharing program – launched in 2009 – has created 180 stations all around the city where you can pick up and drop off bikes. Rates are cheap too – only €1.50 to rent a bike for a day.

Bowling

Crosly Super Bowling
36 Boulevard de l'Empereur (between Grand Place and Place du Sablon), Lower Town. Metro: Gare Centrale. Open Mon–Wed 2pm–1am, Thu 2pm–2am, weekends until midnight. €2.8/person before 6pm; €4 after 6pm. 02 512 08 74. www.crosly.be.
You'll find 25 lanes of bowling bliss here, along with a laser-tag arena, a bar, a restaurant and a café.

Diving

Nemo 33
Rue de Stalle 333, Uccle. Tram 4 or 32: Stalle. 02 332 33 34. www.nemo33.com.

Villo Bikes

©G. Autiquet/www.photolive.be

MUST DO

Eddy "The Cannibal" Merckx

Ask a Belgian who the best cyclist of all time is and they won't stumble in their response: "Eddy Merckx." The Belgian-born cyclist has won every important race out there, earning himself the nickname "The Cannibal" for his insatiable appetite for winning. Merckx won the Tour de France five times, the Giro d'Italia five times, and the Vuelta a España once. He has also won all the monuments of cycling (the oldest and most prestigious one-day races), as well as the world championship. In 1974, Merckx achieved the "Triple Crown" in cycling (Giro d'Italia, the Tour de France and the World Championship Road Race), a feat repeated only one other time, by Stephen Roche in 1987. America's *VeloNews* called him "the greatest and most successful cyclist of all time." You'll be hard-pressed to find a Belgian who disagrees.

Diving in Brussels? When it has the deepest swimming pool in the world, why not?! The 33m/108ft-deep pool is filled with specially filtered non-chlorinated water and has simulated caves and several platforms. Introductory courses for newbies are just €45 and include equipment. Swimmers must be over age 12.

Golf
Royal Golf Course of Belgium
Château de Ravenstein, Tervuren. Tram 44: R-P Ravenstein. Closed Mon. Greens fee €100. 02 767 58 01. www.rgcb.be.
Belgium has some of the oldest golf courses in continental Europe, and the **Royal Golf Course of Belgium**, located in the leafy outskirts of Tervuren, holds one of the highest pedigrees. Founded in 1906 by King Léopold II, the course welcomes non-members during the week (be sure to confirm your reservation).

Rock Climbing
Escalade New Rock
Chaussée de Watermael 136, Auderghem. Metro: Demey. Open Mon–Fri noon–midnight, Sat noon–8pm, Sun noon–11:30pm.

€8.50, €5.50 children under 12. 02 675 17 60.
While the hills of Namur and the Ardennes offer the best outdoor rock climbing, you can practice indoors in Brussels on this 18m/59ft climbing wall. With about 800m²/8,611sq ft of climbing space, New Rock is an ideal place to perfect your technique. Ask about climbing courses and courses for beginners. The "block room" allows a climber to ascend without a rope. No worries, there are large foam rubber mattresses to catch you if you fall.

Skating
Belgium Rollers
Place Poelaert, Palace of Justice, Upper Town. Metro: Louise. Open Jun–Sept, Fri 8pm.
For some years now, Friday nights between June and September bring out Brussels' high rollers – roller-bladers, that is! Hundreds of skaters gather at Place Poelaert every week to enjoy a roll through the capital along 10km/6.25mi of traffic-free streets. Participation is free; you just need skates (for safety reasons, the event is cancelled if it rains).

Patinoire Poseldon

Avenue des Vaillants 4, Woluwé-St-Lambert. Metro: Tomberg. Open Sept–Apr Mon–Fri, 8:30am–5pm, Sat 10am–6p & 8pm–11pm, Sun 10am–6pm. Skate rental €5. 02 762 16 33. www.skate-poseidon.be.

With its large skating rink and retractable roof, a Thursday-evening disco, and an area for the littlest skaters, the Poseidon rink has been attracting Brussels families for decades.

Ice-Skating in the City

Bordered by Quai à la Chaux, Quai au Bois à Bruler, and Quai aux Briques, Lower Town. Metro: Ste-Catherine. €6.

In December, an open-air ice rink fills the site of the Marché aux Poisson adjacent to Place Ste-Catherine during the **Christmas Market** *(see Calendar of Events)*. Skating here is a festive holiday tradition.

Skiing

In winter, downhill and cross-country enthusiasts head to the rolling Ardennes with its dozens of ski stations. But if you get the itch earlier or just can't get away, Brussels has an option.

Yeti Ski

Olympische Dreef 1, Anderlecht. Metro: Eddie Merckx. Check website for hours. Skiing €7.50/hr; snowboarding €10/hr. Rental of equipment €5. 02 520 77 57. www.yetiski.be.

It's not the Alps or even snow for that matter. This synthetic ski hill is designed to simulate the feel of a real snow-covered hill, allowing you to practice your parallels and perfect your technique before you hit the slopes farther afield.

Swimming & Tennis

Sportcity

Avenue Salomé 2, Woluwé-St-Pierre. Tram 39: Rue au Bois. Open year-round daily 8am–7pm. Pool entry €3,50. 02 773 18 20. www.sportcity-woluwe.be.

Ice-skating at the Christmas Market

©Eric Danhier/visitbrussels.be

🚴 Belgian Grand Prix

The town of **Spa** is known for its soothing thermal baths *(see Excursions)*, but this place revs up in August when the Belgian Grand Prix roars into town. Since 1925, Spa and the nearby Spa-Francorchamps Race Course have lured Formula 1 drivers from around the world. Many claim it is the most challenging race on the circuit, thanks to the menacing twists and curves. Spa Francorchamps has also become well known for its unpredictable weather, and at one point in the race's long history, it rained at the Grand Prix 20 years in a row. Racers tour the high-adrenaline 7km/4mi track 44 times, before champagne rains down upon the victor. Race day is on Sunday, but there are qualifying races on Friday and Saturday that will vibrate the soles of your shoes. For schedules, check online at www.belgium-grand-prix.com *(see Calendar of Events)*.

This community sports center in Woluwé-St-Pierre boasts more than 35 different sports. Tennis courts and squash courts can be rented by the hour, and the Olympic-sized pool and a waterslide is a hit with kids. There is a café, and a sport shop where you can buy a bathing cap – required to enter the pool.

V.U.B.
Boulevard de la Plaine 2, Ixelles. Metro: Delta. Pool closed weekends. €3. 02 629 23 11. www.vub.ac.be.
The Free University of Brussels allows non-students to swim in the school's 25m/82ft pool, as well as use their sports facility. The latter boasts indoor soccer, tennis, badminton and a gym. There's also an outdoor running track and a soccer field.

Walking & Running
Brussels Park★, the **Cambre Woods★**, **Tervuren Park★** and the **Sonian Forest★★** are just a few places where walkers and joggers can enjoy miles of traffic-free paths *(see Parks and Gardens)*. Sportcity and VUB also have running tracks.

SPECTATOR SPORTS
Don't feel like participating? Come cheer on your favorite team; there are games galore to watch.

Cycling
The **Tour of Flanders** is held the first Sunday in April in the Ardennes *(www.rvv.be)*, and the **Grand Prix Eddy Merckx** is held in Brussels at the King Baudouin Stadium *(Avenue de Marathon 135/2; Metro: Roi Baudouin)* on the last Sunday in August.

Soccer
🚴 RSC Anderlecht
Avenue Theo Verbeek 2, Anderlecht. Metro: St-Guidon. 02 529 40 67. www.rsca.be.
The Royal Sporting Club Anderlecht, usually referred to simply as Anderlecht, is a Belgian professional soccer (called football in Europe) club based in the Brussels commune of Anderlecht. Their regular appearance in the Champions League makes game days around the Constant Vanden Stock Stadium wildly popular, and a little wild.

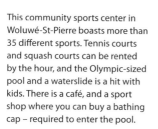

THE GREAT OUTDOORS

PERFORMING ARTS

Brussels is more than just chocolate and beer. Step up to the ticket window of the numerous performing-arts venues in Brussels and you'll enjoy an entertaining array of dance, music, and other performances that will tempt more than your taste buds.

Théâtre de la Monnaie★

Place de la Monnaie, Rue Léopold 4, Lower Town. Metro: De Brouckère. Open Sept–Jun. 070 23 39 39. www.lamonnaie.be.

The home of the National Opera of Belgium takes the name of its theater. Thus, de Munt (Flemish) and La Monnaie (French) refer both to the building as well as the opera company. Dance, ballet and concerts also take place here. The current edifice, designed by architect Joseph Poelaert, is the third theater on the site.

Ancienne Belgique

Boulevard Anspach 110, Lower Town. Metro: De Brouckère. Doors open an hour before concert time. 02 548 24 84. www.abconcerts.be.

This well-respected concert venue consists of three halls, the largest of which has a capacity of 2,000 people. It is considered as one of the best concert halls in Belgium, thanks to its outstanding acoustic qualities. Local and international groups perform year-round here,

and Ancienne Belgique is the first pop/rock venue to receive recognition as a "Grote Vlaamse Cultuurinstelling" – a key cultural organization in Flanders – a title shared with the Flemish Opera and the Museum for Contemporary Art in Antwerp.

BOZAR

Rue Ravenstein 23, Lower Town. Metro: Gare Centrale. 02 507 82 00. www.bozar.be.

Music, theater, cinema, dance, literature, art, photography – BOZAR is a total experience, all under one roof at Brussels' premier cultural venue. Year-round exhibitions and events are held in the beautiful building designed by renowned architect Victor Horta. BOZAR is also home to the **National Orchestra of Belgium** and the **Philharmonic Society**, which plays with some of the world's major orchestras and performers. BOZAR hosts the finals of the **Queen Elisabeth Music Competition**, a rigorous event for violinists, vocalists, pianists and composers. The name BOZAR derives from the French pronunciation of *Beaux-Arts*.

Flagey

Place Ste-Croix, Upper Town. Tram 81 or 83: Flagey. Box office open Mon–Fri 5pm–10pm. 02 641 10 20. www.flagey.be.

Touring Tip

Every Saturday at noon from September to June, visitors can tour the **Théâtre de la Monnaie**. Buy tour tickets from the box office *(open Tue–Sat 11am–6pm; €5,50)*.

Le Botanique

©Latinis/visitbrussels.be

The former home of the Belgian Radio Broadcasting Institute next to Place Flagey is now an exceptional venue with two concert halls and a cinema, accented by an agenda full of events for both adults and children.

Forest National (Vorst)

Avenue Victor Rousseau 208, Forest. Tram 97, 82 or 32: Zaman-Forest National. Box office open daily 8am–10pm. 09 006 95 00. www.forestnational.be.

Somewhat of a metal and concrete eyesore, Brussels' largest indoor venue for major events can accommodate 11,000 for concerts, sporting matches and other spectacles. Despite its name, there are no trees in the immediate vicinity of Forest National.

Halles de Schaerbeek

Rue Royale Ste Marie 22b, Schaerbeek. Metro: Botanique. 02 218 21 07. www.halles.be.

Built in 1865 as a covered market, the original riveted iron and glass structure was ravaged by fire in 1898. Nearly 100 years later, activists from the commune petitioned to turn the abandoned market building into a cultural and performing-arts center for the community. Renovated in 1997, the Halles now boasts two performance halls that welcome dance, music and theater. La Ruelle, formerly the butter and cheese market, is now the access route to both halls.

Le Botanique

Rue Royale 236, St-Josse. Metro: Botanique. Open daily 10am–6pm. 02 218 37 32. www.botanique.be.

Known to locals as Le Bota, this former Botanical Garden turned cultural center boasts concerts, exhibitions and other

Discount Tickets

Arsène 50, the initiative of the Foundation for the Arts, offers half-price same-day tickets for a variety of shows, including jazz, opera, dance and theater. The box office, located at the **Brussels Info Point** *(Rue Royale 2–4; www.arsene50.be)* is open Tuesday to Saturday, from 12:30pm to 5:30pm.

PERFORMING ARTS

117

performances in various rooms and halls onsite. They also own the 2,000-seat concert hall **Cirque Royale** (*Rue de L'Enseignement 81; www.cirque-royal.org*), where larger shows are staged.

Maison du Spectacle – la Bellone

Rue de Flandre 46, Lower Town. Metro: Ste-Catherine. Open Jan–Jun & Aug–Dec, Tue–Fri noon–6pm. Closed July & public holidays. 02 513 33 33. www.bellone.be.

Named for Bellona, the goddess of war, this late-17C residence (not visible from the street) houses exhibitions about the world of performing arts. The striking façade was built in the 18C by Jean Cosyn, architect of the Grand Place, and opens onto a courtyard covered with a glass roof. The venue's once-private theater now hosts workshops as well as music and dance performances that are open to the public.

Royal Conservatory of Music

Rue de la Régence 30, Upper Town. Tram 94 or 92: Petit Sablon. 02 513 45 87. www.conservatoire.be.

Near peaceful Egmont Park and the Place du Petit Sablon, the Royal Conservatory of Music attracts students from all over the world. In spring, fall and winter, a full schedule of matinee and evening concerts are held here in the 19C concert hall.

Royal Flemish Theater
(Koninklijke Vlaamse Schouwburg)

Quai aux Pierres de Taille 9, Lower Town. Metro: Yser. Box office open Tue–Fri noon–7pm, Sat 5pm–7pm. 02 210 11 12. www.kvs.be.

The Flemish Royal Theater – also known as the KVS – stages professional-quality Dutch-speaking theater, with players from Belgium and abroad. Also on stage here are international dance troupes, poetry readings and music performances. The theater hosts occasional exhibitions too, in particular photography.

Théâtre de Marionnettes de Toone

Rue du Marchè aux Herbes 66, Lower Town. Metro: Bourse or Gare Centrale. Closed Jan. 02 511 71 37. www.toone.be.

This beloved theater is more than a puppet playhouse, it's an institution that spans more than 175 years of Brussels history. By day, the theater is a popular pub; by night, talented puppeteers put on delightful performances in French, Dutch, English, Italian and German. In Brussels dialect, "Toone" is the diminutive of the name Antoine, and the theater takes its name from Antoine "Toone" Genty *(see sidebar, below)*.

Théâtre de Poche

Chemin du Gymnase 1a, Bois de la Cambre. Tram 7 or 94: Legrand. 02 649 17 27. www.poche.be.

Located in the beautiful **Bois de la Cambre★**, this little-known "pocket theater" was founded

Play Me a Toone

During the reign of Philippe II, traditional theaters were ordered closed when actors satirically criticized their Spanish ruler. However, in the basements of the Marolles, the people of Brussels replaced the actors with wooden puppets whose biting dialogue continued to revolt against the Spanish. Antoine Genty (Toone I; "Toone" is the Flemish diminutive of Antoine) started his theater in 1830. It passed from generation to generation until 1963 when Toone VI, Pierre Welleman, old and ill, closed the doors of the city's last puppet theater. **Théâtre Toone** was resurrected in 1966 by José Géal, Toone VII, who began a new generation of puppet shows off the Petite Rue des Bouchers. His son took over as Toone VIII in 2003, and the tradition lives on.

by Roger Domani in 1951. In its early days, the theater brought the works of then-unknown – playwrights such as Ionesco, Genet and Audiberti to the stage. Since then, it has continued to feature avant-garde socio-political dramas.

Théâtre Marni

Rue de Vergnies, 25B, Upper Town. Tram 81: Flagey. Box office open Tue–Sat 8pm–2am. 02 639 09 80. www.theatermarni.com.

Just a stone's throw from Place Flagey, this theater is known for its jazz performances but also offers a range of other cultural delights including theater, dance, world music, and events for children.

Théâtre National

Boulevard Emile Jacqmain 111-115, Lower Town. Metro: De Brouckère. Box office open Tue–Sat 11am–6pm. 02 203 41 55. www.theaternational.be.

Since Brussels is a bilingual city, it has two national theaters. This one is the Francophone counterpart of the Royal Flemish Theater or Koninklijke Vlaamse Schouwburg (KVS) and puts on performances in French only,

drawing both classical and contemporary repertoires.

Théâtre Royal du Parc

Rue de la Loi 3, Upper Town. Metro: Parc. 02 505 30 30. www.theaterduparc.be.

Located in **Brussels Park★**, the Théâtre Royal du Parc was built in 1782 and after more than a century of existence, this little venue retains a big presence on Brussels' cultural landscape. A program of some five plays per year run here from September to May. Tickets start at just €5.

Théâtre Royal du Parc

©Simon Shepheard/age fotostock

SHOPPING

Brussels does not come immediately to mind as a European shopping destination, but venture into the various neighborhoods of the city and you might move it to the top of your must-shop list. This old capital will delight antiques lovers, comic-book aficionados, avant-garde fashionistas and, of course, chocoholics.

SHOPPING STREETS AND DISTRICTS

Galeries St-Hubert★★

Rue des Bouchers, between rue du Marché-aux-Herbes & rue de l'Ecuyer, Lower Town. Tram: Bourse. Stores generally open Mon–Sat 10am–6pm. 02 513 89 40. www.galeries-saint-hubert.com.

Opened in 1847 as the world's first covered shopping galleries, this elegant vaulted shopping arcade is just a few steps from the Grand Place and is the address of many chic boutiques – **Delvaux** *(see p125)* for luxury leather goods; the original Neuhaus chocolate shop – as well as several cafés, and a movie theater. Natural light floods the arcade through the soaring vaulted glass, which is supported by iron girders.

Place du Grand Sablon★

Located between the Palace of Justice and Brussels Park, Lower Town. Metro: Parc or Tram 94 to Petit Sablon.

Aside from being one of the most elegant locations in Brussels, this gorgeous square and its surrounding streets hide dozens of antiques shops selling everything from African art to Art Deco desks. On Saturday and Sunday, you'll find an **antiques market** in full swing from 9am to 6pm. The Place du Grand Sablon is also the location of some of Belgium's best-known chocolate shops, including **Pierre Marcolini**, **Wittamer** and **Neuhaus** *(see p124)*.

Avenue Louise and Boulevard de Waterloo

South of Center. Metro: Louise.

Top-name international brands from Gucci to Louis Vuitton to BMW spread out from the intersection of Avenue Louise and Boulevard de Waterloo. Count on high-end shops with matching price tags. **Rue de Joncker** and **Rue Jean Stas** are two pedestrian streets that intersect Avenue Louise and offer outdoor dining and more unique boutiques.

Galeries St-Hubert

© Marcel Vanhulst/visitbrussels.be

MUST DO

120

Les Marolles

Below the Place du Grand Sablon, Lower Town. Tram 92 or 94: Petit Sablon. Stores are generally open Sun but closed Mon.

Snuggled up against the **Church of Our Lady of the Chapel**, Les Marolles is a typical working-class neighborhood of Brussels and one of the few areas of the city where you might still hear the old Bruxellois dialect. The area, with its two main streets – the parallel **Rue Haute** and **Rue Blaes** – contains an eclectic mix of antiques stores, designer furniture and art galleries, with cafés and restaurants tucked in-between. Les Marolles is famous for the daily flea market held on the Place du Jeu de Balle *(see sidebar, below)*.

Place Brugmann

Between Rue de Bailli and St-Gilles. Tram 92: Darwin. Most stores closed Sun.

For a real taste of local color, wander the streets that intersect this quiet square and its residential neighborhood south of the city center. You'll be charmed by elegant

boutiques like **Graphie Sud** *(Rue Berkendael 195)*, **Claude Hontoir** *(no. 14)*, and **Les Précieuses** *(no. 20)*. The popular **Winery** wine bar *(no. 18; see Nightlife)* and **Balmoral** *(no. 21)*, an authentic American-style diner, are also mainstays. **Gaudron** *(no. 3)*, a delightful gourmet grocer with a take-out counter, is a lunchtime favorite.

Rue Antoine Dansaert

Between The Bourse and the Brussels-Charleroi canal, Lower Town. Metro: Bourse. Stores are generally open Mon–Sat 11am–6pm. Closed Sunday.

Trendy and always buzzing, this street is known as the place to shop for cutting-edge Belgian fashions. Look for names like Christophe Coppens, Annemie Verbeke and Olivier Strelli. The boutique **Stijl** is also located here; they sell collections from the famous Antwerp designers who put Belgian fashion on the international radar. Brands sold at Stijl include Ann Demeulemeester, Raf Simons, Dries van Noten and Kris van Assche.

Treasure Hunting

In a city often overshadowed by tony department stores and touristy boutiques, the best digging around is often done at the flea market – called the **Vieux Marché** – on the **Place du Jeu de Balle** in Les Marolles. A little bit garage sale and a whole lot of fun, this market takes place every day, rain or shine, and is the oldest of its kind in Brussels. Dig through the piles of estate-sale items ranging from useful (clothes) to useless (warped vinyl records and a giant bust of Bart Simpson). You can even find the proverbial kitchen sink, should you be in the market for one. Vendors start selling their goods as early as 6am and professional flea-market hounds arrive early for one-of-a-kind finds. Near the end of the day (2pm), leftovers can be bargained down to a steal.

Rue du Bailli

Between Avenue Louise and Trinity Church, Châtelain. Tram 94: Bailli. Stores generally open Mon–Sat 10am–6pm. Closed Sun.

This commercial street near Place du Châtelain feels like a village within the city, and it hides a plethora of cafés, bars, restaurants and shops. Among the favorites are the discount **Dod** stores, featuring last season's designer labels at reduced prices. The Wednesday afternoon Market on Place du Châtelain *(opposite)* is popular with locals.

Rue Neuve

Lower Town. Metro: Rogier. Stores are generally open Mon–Sat 10am–6pm. Closed Sun.

In the city center, Rue Neuve is one of the busiest shopping streets in all of Belgium. Stretching between Place de la Monnaie and Place Charles Rogier, the avenue is lined mostly with chain stores (Esprit, Hema, Zara, H&M) as well as the large department store **Inno** *(no. 11)*. Here you'll also find the indoor shopping center **City 2** *(no. 123)*,

housing more clothing stores and a gigantic outpost of **Fnac**, the French media superstore. During sale periods *(see sidebar, p124)*, be prepared to be jostled by crowds along this pedestrian-only street.

MARKETS

Brussels is a city of neighborhood markets, and there is no shortage of them to be found every day of the week, somewhere around the city. Make time to savor one or more of these outdoor emporiums.

Daily

Place Ste-Catherine has long been a local favorite for produce, fish, flowers and the scenic surrounds. *Metro: Ste-Catherine. Open 7am–5pm.*

Place du Jeu de Balle is Brussels' oldest flea market. *Metro: Porte de Hal. Open 7am–2pm.*

The century-old **Mabru** market is renowned for its national and international products. It's also the preferred market for chefs in Brussels. *Quai des Usines 22/23. Tram 3: Mabru. Open Mon, Wed, Fri 3pm–10pm; Tue, Thu, Sat 1pm–10pm.*

Belgian Six-Pack

Belgian fashion has a following all its own, thanks in part to a group of innovative designers known as **The Antwerp Six**. The members of this group – Ann Demeulemeester, Dirk Bikkembergs, Dirk Van Saene, Dries van Noten, Marina Yee and Walter Van Beirendonck – all graduated from the now-famous Antwerp Royal Academy of Fine Arts, an institution (known as "The Antwerp Academy") with a reputation for turning out inventive and technically savvy designers. In the 1980s, the Antwerp Six hired a truck, stuffed their collections in the back, and high-tailed it to London for Fashion Week. They took the town by storm, forever earning a place in fashion history, and paving the way for future avant-garde designers from Belgium, many of whom have shops in Antwerp and along Rue Antoine Dansaert in Brussels.

Flea market on the Place du Jeu de Balle
©Julian Love/Apa Publications

Monday

Place Van Meenen in St-Gilles is the site of an afternoon food market, featuring plenty of free tastes in front of the stunning Maison Communale de St-Gilles. *Metro: Horta. Open 12:30pm–7pm.*

Tuesday

Place Dumon, in the residential area of Woluwé-St-Pierre, holds a pleasant and varied market on Tuesday, Friday and Saturday. People line up for the hot waffles sold here. *Metro: Stockel. Open 7am–2pm.*

Wednesday

Place du Châtelain in the Ixelles neighborhood is a gourmet-lovers' market, as well as a good place for an after-work apéritif. *Tram 94: Bailli. Open 2pm–8pm.*

Friday–Saturday

On **Place du Grand Sablon★**, an antiques market takes place on the square every weekend. *Tram 94: Petit Sablon.Open Sat–Sun, 9am–6pm.*
Anderlecht Market *(Rue Ropsy-Chaudron 24)*, called the Abbatoir market for its locale on the site of a former slaughterhouse, welcomes nearly 80,000 visitors each weekend. *Metro: Delacroix. Open 7am–3pm.*

Sunday

🚲 **Midi Market** *(at the Gare du Midi, Rue de France 40)*, Brussels' largest market, is popular for its Middle Eastern and North African specialties, among myriad other offerings. *Metro: Gare du Midi. Open 6am–1pm.*
Place Jourdan, in the European Quarter, hosts a Sunday morning market teeming with flowers, food, clothes, candy and more. *Metro: Schuman. Open 7am–2pm.*

SHOPPING BY SUBJECT

🍴 **Belgian Gourmet Specialties**
Beermania
Chaussée de Wavre 174, Upper Town. Metro: Porte de Namur. Open Mon–Sat 11am–9pm. 02 512 17 88. www.beermania.be.
The name says it all, and with more than 400 varieties of Belgium's favorite elixir (and matching glasses to boot) under one roof,

this shop near the European Quarter may end up being your first and last call of the night.

Dandoy

Rue au Beurre 31, Lower Town. Metro: Bourse. Open Mon–Sat, 8:30am–7pm, Sun, 10:30am–7pm. 02 511 03 26. www.biscuiterie dandoy.be.

Butter Street seems a fitting address for this traditional family business, which has been baking handcrafted **biscuits** since 1829. Dandoy's most famous treat is the irresistible spice cookie called *Speculaas*. At Christmastime the cookie, molded into the form of St. Nicholas, is a popular gift – especially on December 6 when

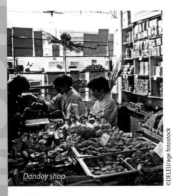

Dandoy shop

©DELEU/age fotostock

Sinterklaas leaves *Speculaas* in the shoes of good boys and girls.

🍫 Chocolate

Chocolatier Mary

Rue Royale 73, Upper Town. Metro: Parc or Tram 92 or 94 to Congrès. Open Mon–Sat 10am–6pm. 02 217 45 00. www.mary choc.com.

Madame Marie Dellue opened her first chocolate shop on Rue Royale in 1919 and quickly earned a reputation for artisanal quality. Almost a century later, chocolatiers here still follow Mary's recipes. Lick your lips on a factory tour or sign up for a workshop to learn the art of making chocolate.

Neuhaus

Galerie de la Reine 2–27, Lower Town. Metro: Gare Centrale. Open Mon–Sat 10am–8pm. 02 512 63 59. www.neuhaus.be.

Jean Neuhaus, a Swiss immigrant, founded this company in Brussels in 1857. He opened his first store in the elegant **Galeries St-Hubert★★**, which you can still visit today. His grandson, Jean Neuhaus II, invented the first filled chocolate, called the **praline**. Three years later, he created the decorative box, or *ballotin*, to protect his delicate candies.

Pierre Marcolini

Rue de Minimes 1, Lower Town. Metro: Parc or Tram 94 to Petit Sablon. Open Tue–Sat 10am–6pm. 02 514 12 06. www.marcolini.be.

In a country famed for chocolate, Pierre Marcolini has cast himself as the *haute couturier* of the confection. He launched his first store in Brussels in 1995, the same year he was named the World

Pêle-Mêle
Boulevard Maurice Lemonnier 55,
Lower Town. Metro: Anneessens.
Open Mon–Sat 10am–6:30pm.
02 548 78 00. www.pele-mele.be.
Browse new and used comics, CDs, DVDs, toys, and other items sure to please comics enthusiasts.

Luxury Leather Goods
Delvaux
Boulevard de Waterloo 27,
Upper Town. Metro: Louise.
Open Mon–Sat 10am–6pm.
02 513 05 05. www.delvaux.com.
The oldest luxury-leather-goods company in the world is Belgian? That's right, and it's in Brussels. In 1829, the company's founder, Charles Delvaux, started producing quality travel trunks by hand in his Brussels studio.
Soon after, the company became a supplier to the Belgian royal court. Some 100 years later, the company still prides itself on producing fine handcrafted leather goods and made-to-order personal items. Stop into the two-level shop near Avenue Louise to see the latest handbag styles.

Postcards
Plaizier Art Shop
Rue des Éperonniers 50,
Lower Town. Metro: Gare Centrale.
Open Mon–Sat, 11am–6pm.
Closed Sun. 02 513 47 30.
www.plaizier.be.
Forget about the zillions of typical postcards you'll flip through in kitschy tourist shops, and head to this unique boutique. Inside you'll find a wealth of artistic and historical images of the city of Brussels that are well worth holding onto as keepsakes, or sticking on the refrigerator door.

Neuhaus chocolate shop

©Marcel Vanhulst/visitbrussels.be

Champion of Pastry. In his flagship shop on the Place du Grand Sablon, little chocolate gems tempt you behind the glass.

Wittamer
Place du Grand Sablon 12,
Lower Town. Metro: Parc or Tram
94 to Petit Sablon. Open Mon 9am–
6pm, Tue–Thu 7am–7pm, Sun 7am
–6:30pm. 02 512 37 42.
www.wittamer.com.
The Wittamer family have been making chocolate in this location since 1910. Get your goodies to go in the boutique or head upstairs to enjoy the confections in the charming tearoom overlooking the square.

Comics
Le Dépôt de Bruxelles
Rue du Midi 108, Lower Town.
Metro: Bourse. Open Mon–Sat
11am–6:30pm. 02 513 04 84.
www.depotbd.com.
Albums, objects, rare items and everything else connected to "BD" (*bande dessinée*, French for "comic strip") is sold at this shop, which has been around since 1984.

NIGHTLIFE

Whether you are searching for a little night music, or just want a nightcap, there is plenty to please night owls in every neighborhood of Brussels. The areas around Place St-Géry and the Grand Place★★★ are particularly lively after dark.

Live Music and Dancing

L'Archiduc
Rue Antoine Dansaert 6, Lower Town. Metro: Bourse. Open daily 4pm–5am. 02 512 06 52. www.archiduc.net.

A veteran on the Brussels nightlife landscape, the Art Deco bar is noted for its cool speakeasy vibe, its cocktails and its live jazz music. On Saturdays, drop off those packages and come for Jazz after Shopping from 5pm to 7pm.

Booze 'n Blues
Rue des Riches Claires 20, Lower Town. Metro: Bourse. 02 513 93 33.

Just steps from Place St-Géry, this blues bar is famous for its loaded jukebox, crafted cocktails, and enthusiastic patrons who come to stay and dance until dawn.

Café Maison du Peuple
Parvis de St-Gilles 39, St-Gilles. Metro: De Brouckère. 02 850 09 08. www.maison-du-peuple.be.

A range of activities, from monthly art exhibitions to live local bands, entertain day and night at this café/bar, which takes its name from the 1907 building it occupies.

Churchill's
Rue de l'Ecuyer 29, Lower Town. Metro: De Brouckère. 02 514 27 10. www.churchills.be.

English owned and operated, Churchill's features live music every Friday and Saturday starring some of Belgium's best bands. Three big-screen TVs guarantee you won't miss your favorite sports team.

Havana
Rue de l'Epée 4, Lower Town. Metro: Louise or Tram 94 to Poelaert (take the elevator down from Place Poelaert). 02 502 12 24. www.havana-brussels.com.

With two dance floors, four bars, live music, and DJs, Havana is definitely where night life sizzles – until 5am on Friday and all night on Saturday.

Café Maison du Peuple

©Giotto Agency/Café Maison du Peuple

MUST DO

Brussels "Champagne"

Made for centuries in and around Brussels, **Lambic beer** is a wheat beer fermented from yeast naturally present in the air of the Senne Valley of Brussels, rather than from yeast added by the brewer. The result is a bubbly and tart elixir. Lambics are blended to create a variant called Gueuze, which is still brewed at **Timmermans** *(Kerkstraat 11, Itterbeek; www.anthonymartin.be)*. Cherry-flavored Lambic, called Kriek, is another popular and tasty variation.

Magic Mirrors

Place Ste-Catherine, Lower Town. Metro: Ste-Catherine. 04 75 53 42 80. www.magicmirrors.com.

The address – "behind the church on Place Ste-Catherine" – adds to the mysterious glamour of this former 1920s circus tent, which re-creates the European mirror tents of the late 19C. Magic Mirrors has become the city's most exquisite bar and live-music venue.

Mezzo Bar

Rue Borgval 18, Lower Town. Metro: Bourse. 02 646 56 94. www.mezzo.be.

There is a homey feel to this bar located near the always-abuzz Place St-Géry. On the weekend, DJs take over and spin all night long – until breakfast time (Mezzo is open until 7am Friday and Saturday).

Roskam

Rue de Flanders 9, Lower Town. Metro: Ste-Catherine or Bourse. 02 503 51 54.

Lively Rue de Flandre, between Rue Antoine Dansaert and Place Ste-Catherine, sees a steady stream of locals hoofing it to this salt-of-the-earth bar, where inexpensive beer and a regular lineup of guitar pluckers are *de rigueur*. Plan to stay late; Roskam is open until 4am Friday and Saturday, and until 2am the rest of the week.

Wine Bars and Beer Pubs

A La Morte Subite

Rue Montagne-aux-herbes Potagère 7, Lower Town. Metro: Gare Centrale. 02 513 13 18. alamortsubite.com.

This bar, adorned with 1928 architectural details, is a must-try for Gueuze and Lambic beer.

A La Bécasse

Rue de Tabora 11, Lower Town. Metro: Bourse. 02 511 00 06. www.alabecasse.com.

Serving a large variety of Belgian and imported beer, A La Bécasse is one of the oldest pubs in Brussels.

Oeno TK

Rue Africaine 29–31 (behind the church), Châtelain. Tram 81: Trinité. 02 534 64 34. www.oenotk.be.

Expect a wide selection of affordable wines from around the world at this casual spot, which is set at the end of Rue de Bailli.

Winery

Place G. Brugmann 18. Tram 92: Darwin. 02 345 47 17. www.wineryonline.be.

Locals come to this popular neighborhood wine bar for good wine in a mellow setting.

SPAS

Spa – the name itself comes from the eponymous Belgian town in the Ardennes known for its thermal baths. But if you can't manage to get there, any of these day spas in and around Brussels will make your tired muscles and travel stress a thing of the past.

Aspria
Place Wiltcher, Avenue Louise 71B. Metro: Louise or Tram 94 to Stéphanie. 02 610 40 66. www.aspria-avenuelouise.be.
This spa chain can be found in Europe's finest cities and is continually ranked among the continent's best health clubs. The Avenue Louise branch is an exclusive and exceptional hideaway, with a steam room, a Jacuzzi, an indoor pool and a fitness center. All treatments here are available for both women and men.

Body Minute
Rue du Bailli 32, Châtelain. Tram 81 or 94: Bailli. Closed Mon. 02 647 65 67. www.bodyminute.be.

For a quickie wax or mani-pedi, this women-only walk-in spa is just the ticket to get you in tip-top shape, ASAP. Buy a monthly membership, and enjoy low prices for any service.

Livia Kova
Rue d'Idalie 12, Upper Town. Metro: Porte de Namur or Trône. 02 280 43 29. www.liviakova.com.
This spa has garnered local awards for good reason. Pampering is the name of the game here, with relaxing rituals like Cleopatra's Secret, which nourishes skin with special vitamins and minerals; and the stress-busting Bio-Zen ritual that focuses on relaxing both the body and mind.

Monsieur K
Rue Antoine Dansaert 115, Lower Town. Metro: Ste-Catherine. 02 503 55 25. www.monsieur-k.be.
Finally, a spa just for men! Come discover the pleasures of an exclusive range of peels, facials, micro-dermabrasion, body scrubs, massages, and products tailored to the masculine sex.

Serendip Spa
Place Stéphanie 18, Upper Town. Metro: Louise or Tram 94 to Stéphanie. 02 503 55 04. www.serendipspa.com.
Herbal teas, soothing music and a meditation lounge mark this Avenue Louise outpost of tranquility. Indulgent rituals with

Spasiba
©Spasiba

MUST DO

The Origins of Spas

The earliest spa treatments are associated with balneotherapy, or treating disease using the curative properties of mineral waters, a belief that goes back to prehistoric times. It was the Romans, however, who elevated bathing to an art form, by developing a bathing ritual that included a massage and a rest after the bath. The term "spa" derives from the small Belgian town of the same name (see Excursions), a popular "watering hole" since Roman times, when the location was called Aquae Spadanae.

enticing names like Complete Surrender (incorporating a warm foot bath, a massage and a lifting finger-tip facial) are the hallmarks of this reputable day spa, which also includes a yoga studio upstairs.

Spasiba
Boulevard de Waterloo 47b, Upper Town. Metro: Louise. Closed Mon. 02 514 15 33. www.spasiba.be.
Whether you want to soak in a scented tub surrounded by candles or you desire a full-body massage, this tranquil oasis is a great place to spend a day. Hot-stone messages, wraps, scrubs and balneotherapy (mineral water treatments), for one or two, will enhance your feeling of well-being in no time. Spa rituals here take their cues from the Far East, Morocco and India.

Zeïn Oriental Spa
Avenue du Port 86c, Schaerbeek. Metro: Ribacourt. 02 424 35 22. www.zeinorientalspa.be.
Located in the historic Tour & Taxis building, this urban Zen outpost is known for its hammam (Turkish baths), but you can indulge in Moroccan-inspired massages and facials here too, in a beautifully renovated 19C structure.

Spa Excursions

Cinque Mondes Spa
Chaussee de Bruxelles, 135, La Hulpe. 02 290 98 00. www.dolce-la-hulpe-brussels-hotel.com.
Recognized as one of Europe's leading conference and hotel facilities, Dolce La Hulpe (approx. 20km/12.5mi southeast of Brussels), also has a 799m²/8,600sq ft spa with a menu of treatments and massages from around the globe. Located in the heart of a verdant natural setting, Cinque Mondes Spa is the ultimate relaxation station. For exploring the surrounding Sonian Forest, the spa also rents mountain bikes to those adventurous folks who just can't take it easy.

Thermae Grimbergen
Wolvertemsesteenweg, 74, Grimbergen. 02 270 81 96. www.thermae-grimbergen.be.
Boasting a quiet setting in the small town of Grimbergen, just 15 minutes outside Brussels, this Spa-Hotel has thermal baths, a wide variety of beauty treatments, an on-site restaurant and a hotel. Why not make a relaxing weekend of it and go for one of the combination hotel/spa packages?

SPAS

RESTAURANTS

With more than 2,000 restaurants to choose among, Brussels residents have only one problem when it comes to dining out: deciding where to go. Beyond that, count on top-quality cuisine (as long as you steer clear of the main tourist drag, Rue des Bouchers) with prices ranging from inexpensive to stratospheric. Many restaurants offer affordable, set two- or three-course menus, which are especially budget-friendly at lunchtime. As a rule, the Lower Town lays claim to the best places to eat, with the fine seafood establishments in the Ste-Catherine quarter leading the pack. No matter the neighborhood, when the sun is shining, outdoor terraces overflow with locals and visitors taking part in Brussels' favorite pastime – eating.

Prices and Opening Hours

The restaurants in this section were selected for their ambience, location, variety of regional dishes and/or value for money. Prices indicate the average cost of an appetizer, main course and dessert for one person, not including beverages, taxes or surcharges. Most restaurants are open daily (except where noted; many are closed Monday), though they tend to close between lunch and dinner (usually 2pm–7pm). It's also common in Brussels for restaurants, especially the smaller, family-run places, to be closed for several weeks in August. Be sure to check the websites or call before you go. Most (but not all) restaurants accept major credit cards, and American Express is not as widely accepted as Visa and MasterCard.

$ under €16
$$ €16–€30
$$$ €30–€50
$$$$ over €50

Brussels' Specialties

It's almost impossible to eat badly in Brussels, a city that prides itself on the quantity and quality of its restaurants. Aside from beer and Belgian chocolate, here are some

Moules frites

©Arthur Los; Milo-Profi Fotografie/Gent Toerisme

local specialties to add to your must-try list.

Asperges à la Flamande – White asparagus (available fresh May–June) topped with a sauce of chopped hard-boiled eggs, lemon, butter and herbs.

Carbonnade Flamande – A beef and onion stew slow-braised in Belgian beer.

Chicon au gratin – Endive baked with ham and cheese.

Croquettes de crevettes: Fried croquettes, filled with small shrimp and seasoned sauce.

Liège waffle – Sold from trucks or stands on the street, these small doughy waffles are stuffed with chunks of sugar and have a crunchy caramelized crust. Eat them with your hands – no maple syrup needed.

Mitraillette – French for "machine gun," this sandwich overflows with meat, sauce, *frites* and crudités. Find mitraillettes at street vendors' stalls or fry shacks, and don't spare the calories.

Moules frites – The Belgian classic – mussels and French fries – is best eaten when mussels are in season (Aug–Mar).

Speculaas – A traditional Belgian spice cookie that's especially popular at Christmastime.

Stoemp – Mashed potatoes mixed with one or more root vegetables, normally served with a meat such as sausage.

Tomate Crevettes – This typical starter consists of a whole tomato, stuffed with small gray shrimp and topped with mayonnaise.

Waterzooi – This creamy stew of chicken or fish with vegetables originated in Ghent. The name, which means "watery mess," belies its wonderful taste.

Lower Town

ComoComo
$ Spanish
Rue Antoine Dansaert 19.
Metro: Bourse. 02 503 03 03.
www.comocomo.be.
The quirky restaurant has become a huge success and is a launching spot for a fun night out in the capital. Diners sit on both sides of a conveyor belt that snakes through the restaurant and pluck off color-coded plates of Pintxos (tapas) at will. Pay by the number of plates taken and wash it all down with some Spanish wine.

ComoComo

©Tommy de Lange/ComoComo

Le Perroquet
$ Belgian
Rue Watteeu 31. Tram 94: Petit Sablon. 02 512 99 22.
This Art Deco gem on a small street off the Place du Petit Sablon, is busy day and night. It's known for a menu of pita sandwiches stuffed with every imaginable combination, at very affordable prices. Add homemade desserts and Belgian beers, and you'll be moving Le Perroquet to the top of your must-go-again list.

RESTAURANTS

131

Bij den Boer
$$ Seafood
Quai aux Briques, 60. Metro: Ste-Catherine. 02 512 61 22. www.bijdenboer.com. Closed Sun.
A favorite spot for *moules-frites*, this popular fish restaurant just off Place Ste-Catherine serves up fabulously fresh seafood and proposes a four-course weekly menu for only €27.50.

Bleu de Toi
$$ Belgian
Rue des Alexiens 73. Metro: Gare Centrale. 02 502 43 71. www.bleudetoi.be. Closed Sun. No lunch Sat; no dinner Mon.
Belgium's love affair with the potato goes way beyond French fries at this unassuming place, where the star of the show is the *bintje*, a potato variety developed in the Netherlands. Here, the mighty spud becomes the *plat de résistance* when stuffed with lobster, crab, vegetables, meat, cheese, caviar and more.

©Bleu de Toi
Bleu de Toi

Fanny Thai
$$ Thai
Rue Jules Van Praet 36. Metro: Bourse. 02 502 64 22. www.fanny-thai.be.
Boasting authentic Thai and Vietnamese specialties, this

subdued restaurant with friendly and efficient service sits in the heart of the trendy St-Géry area. Calm prevails in the Zen-like interior, where favorites run from fresh spring rolls to spicy curry dishes. The weekday lunch menu (€8.50) is a steal.

©Kokob

Kokob
$$ Ethiopian
Rue des Grands Carmes 10. Metro: Anneessens. 02 511 19 50. www.kokob.be. No lunch Mon–Wed.
For a new food experience in Brussels, head to this small restaurant not far from the Grand Place for authentic Ethiopian fare. No forks or knives, just a loaf of tear-off bread and a sampling of dishes to tantalize. Most people, especially first-timers, try the Wot – a typical stew of meat and vegetables seasoned with berbere, a spice mix from Ethiopia.

La Brouette
$$ Belgian
Grand Place 2–3. Metro: Gare Centrale or Bourse. 02 511 20 22. www.taverne-brouette.be.
Sure, it's touristy and the service can be surly, but this café in the former guildhall of the *graissiers* (grease makers), serves some of the best food on the Grand Place –

MUST EAT

with a side of stellar views. Service is nonstop from 8am to midnight, making it ideal for a beer or a *flammekuchen* (Flemish-style pizza) any time.

La Kasbah
$$ **Moroccan**
Rue Antoine Dansaert 20. Metro: Bourse. 02 502 40 26. www.lakasbahresto.com.
Park your magic carpet at this Moroccan restaurant on the trendy Rue Antoine Dansaert, where the ceiling dangles with more than 100 multicolored lanterns. This is the place to try a tagine (a Moroccan stew cooked in a clay pot of the same name) accompanied by flatbread and couscous.

La Mer du Nord (De Nordzee)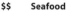
$$ **Seafood**
Rue Ste-Catherine 45 (on the corner of the square). Metro: Ste-Catherine 02 513 11 92. www.vishandel noordzee.be. Closed Mon.
You can't miss the lineup of locals under the blue awning of the Mer du Nord fish bar, a favorite for a fast and fresh lunch. Mussels, fish soup, shrimp, calamari – you name it, they have it. Wash it down with a glass of rosé at the standing-only tables and bar.

Soul
$$ **Contemporary**
Rue de la Samaritaine 20. Tram 92 or 94: Petit Sablon. 02 513 52 13. www.soulresto.com. Dinner only. Closed Mon & Tue.
Organic products are the focus here, most of them free of additives, preservatives and white sugar, as well as butter and cream. The delicious, globally accented

and healthy result yields the likes of salmon carpaccio with an herb, pomegranate and mango salad.

Belga Queen
$$$ **Regional Belgian**
Rue du Fossé aux Loups. Metro: De Brouckère. 02 217 21 87. www.be.lgaqueen.be.
This beauty occupies a former bank building and pays homage to its homeland. From the design to the produce and the long wine list, everything is sourced from Belgian providers. After dinner, check out the cigar bar and jazz club located downstairs in the former bank vaults.

L'Idiot du Village
$$$ **French**
Rue Notre-Seigneur 1. Tram 94: Petit Sablon. 02 502 55 82. Closed weekends.
Far from being the village idiot, as its name would have you believe, this little find in the Marolles district is big on charm and even bigger on hearty food – lovingly served by the same family for more than 15 years.

Lola
$$$ **International**
Place du Grand Sablon 33. Tram 92 or 94: Petit Sablon. 02 514 24 60. www.restolola.be.
As soon as this modern brasserie opened on the Place du Grand Sablon, it became an instant hit. Artfully presented dishes range from steak tartare and lamb confit to chicken curry and pappardelle scampi, and the global wine list slants heavily toward France. Desserts are almost too pretty to eat. Almost.

RESTAURANTS

STEAKfrit'
$$$ Contemporary Belgian
Rue des Dominicains 14. Metro: De Brouckère. 02 229 00 99. www.steakfrit.be. Closed Mon afternoon.

This brasserie, with several branches in the city, whisks a classic Belgian kitchen into modern times. As the name indicates, steak *frites* is a much-ordered item, as are shrimp croquettes and tomatoes stuffed with shrimp. Try it for a quick bite, an afternoon coffee, or drink at the bar, which is open all day.

Tavern du Passage
$$$ Belgian
Galerie de la Reine 30. Metro: Gare Centrale. 02 512 37 31. www.taverne-du-passage.be.
Under the glass roof of the Galeries St-Hubert, this Art Deco restaurant serves traditional Belgian specialties like waterzooi, among a variety of other meat, fish and vegetarian dishes. Special lunch menus during the week start at €19, and service is nonstop from midday to midnight.

Comme Chez Soi
$$$$ French
Place Rouppe 23. 02 512 29 21. Metro: Anneessens. www.comme chezsoi.be. Closed Sun, Mon & mid-July–mid-Aug.

Comme chez Soi
©Comme chez Soi

Founded in 1926, this elegant institution is regarded by many as the crown jewel of the city's restaurant scene. Signature specialties (think suprêmes of pigeon with green cardamom) here have held their own over four generations, complemented by the updated creations of Chef Lionel Rigolet. A destination in itself, Comme Chez Soi is still *the* Brussels table to secure.

Sea Grill Yves Mattagne
$$$$ Seafood
Rue du Fossé aux Loups 47. Metro: Gare Centrale or De Brouckère. 02 212 08 00. www.seagrill.be. Closed Sat, Sun & mid-July–mid-Aug.
Hailed as one of the most highly acclaimed restaurants in Brussels, this luxurious spot in the Radisson Blu Royal Hotel *(see MUST STAY)* recently received a facelift. Now soft colors and modern style set the scene for the ambitious fish and shellfish menu expertly executed by Chef Yves Mattagne. Roasted turbot with oyster béarnaise, and lobster prepared tableside, will give you an idea of the stellar fare.

Upper Town

El Vergel
$ Latin American
Rue du Trône 39. Metro: Trône. 02 502 69 30. www.elvergel.be. Open 8am–3pm. Closed weekends. Dinner Thu only.
Latin American cuisine was hard to find in Brussels, until El Vergel came to town in 2005. Blending Latin American spices with Mediterranean recipes, the restaurant has earned a cult-like

following. Fresh ingredients go into tacos, tostadas and empanadas, as well as specialties like Brazilian beef steak.

🍴 Maison Antoine
$ Belgian
Place Jourdan 1.
Metro: Schuman. 02 230 54 56.
www.maisonantoine.be.
There are dozens of fry shacks all over Brussels, but Maison Antoine remains a favorite potato pilgrimage point for a *cornet* (cone) of the country's most beloved snack (the misnamed French fry is actually a Belgian creation). Lines start forming early.

Mamma Roma
$ Italian
Chaussée de Vleurgat 5.
Tram 81: Flagey. 02 640 42 80.
www.mammaroma.com.
Ask anyone in Brussels where to get the best pizza and chances are they'll say "Mamma Roma." It's always packed at this place, where pizzas are baked fresh and the options *du jour* are displayed behind the counter. Simply point out your pleasure and enjoy.

🍴 Il Pasticcio
$$ Italian
Rue Marie de Bourgogne 3.
Metro: Trône. 02 512 62 52.
Lunch Mon–Fri. Dinner Wed & Fri.
Closed weekends.
Hidden in the European quarter, not far from the Place du Luxembourg, this unassuming Italian restaurant doesn't look like much from the outside, but inside you'll find some of the city's best Italian food, served without pretention or a hefty price tag. Homemade pastas and house wine

Maison Antoine
©Maison Antoine

seem to be the preferred lunch. Arrive early to avoid the noon rush.

L'Ultime Atome
$$ Belgian
Rue St-Boniface 14. Metro:
Porte de Namur. 02 511 13 67.
Wedged between the shopping street Chaussée d'Ixelles and the African quarter of Matongé, Brussels' version of a neighborhood restaurant serves breakfast, lunch and dinner to a constant crowd. The café is equally good as a launching pad for a night on the town or for an after-party Belgian beer.

South of Center

Café de la Presse
$ Café
Avenue Louise 493, Ixelles.
Tram 94: Legrand. 02 649 09 35.
www.cafedelapress.be.
If you're looking for an overstuffed couch to flop on to sip your cappuccino and check your e-mail, or you just want to have a bite to eat that doesn't involve waiters or translation, this easy-going café is the place. No frills yet decidedly hip, Café de la Presse offers ready-made sandwiches and soups, plus a bagel bar. Wi-Fi is free with any purchase.

La Araucana

$$ **South American**

Rue de L'Hôtel des Monnaies 63, St-Gilles. Metro: Hôtel des Monnaies. 02 539 25 76. www.restaurantaraucana.be.

When you tire of Belgian fare and pizza, head to this lively local restaurant (a.k.a. Chez Adela) that is always buzzing, often with live music and dancing. The owner (Adela) is often seen talking to patrons who come not only for the warm welcome, but also for the house specialty, Argentine beef. Other menu options like chili con carne and prawns in garlic oil will add zest to your night.

Les Fils à Papa

$$ **Belgian**

Chaussée de Waterloo 1484, Uccle. Tram 92: Fort Jaco. 02 374 41 44. www.lesfilsapapa.be. Closed Sun. No lunch Sat.

Venture out to Uccle, just beyond the Cambre Woods, and reward yourself at this restaurant, stashed in a historic house that has been renovated and now touts old Hollywood glamour. Walls are bedecked with black-and-white photos of famous men and their sons (a reference to the

Le Chalet Robinson
©Le Chalet Robinson

restaurant's name), while the menu stars traditional Belgian dishes.

La Canne en Ville

$$$ **French**

Rue de la Reforme 22, Ixelles. Tram 92: Ma Campagne. 02 347 29 26. www.lacanneenville.be.

This place feels like an old neighborhood favorite, and one never tires of eating here. Located near the elegant Place Brugmann and housed in an old butcher shop, La Canne en Ville has a small but varied menu of meat, fish and regional specialties. For dessert, go for the *speculaas* ice cream – a real Belgian treat!

La Canne en Ville
©Luc Viatour/La Canne En Ville

Le Chalet Robinson

$$$ **Contemporary Belgian**

Robinson Island, Bois de la Cambre. Tram 7: Longchamps. 02 772 92 92. www.chaletrobinson.be.

On Robinson Island in the middle of the lake in the Cambre Woods, Chalet Robinson is a historical landmark. The likes of sole meuniere and penne with housemade pesto, eaten on the spacious lakeside terrace, make the Chalet worth a detour (reservations suggested). An electric launch takes guests to the island for €1.

MUST EAT

Le Fruit Défendu
$$$ French
Rue Tenbosch 108, Ixelles. Tram 92: Ma Campagne. 02 347 42 47. Closed Sun. No lunch Sat.
Even the name, "the forbidden fruit," conjures up the idea that anything is possible, and in this cozy bistro of dark wood and candlelight, you'll believe in possibilities. Located in a busy restaurant quarter near Place du Châtelain, this place makes a perfect hideaway for a romantic dinner. Creative dishes, beautifully presented, use seasonal products plucked from local markets by chef Pascal Frénot.

Les Brasseries Georges
$$$ French
Avenue Winston Churchill 359, Bois de la Cambre. Tram 3 or 23: Longchamps. 02 347 21 00. www.brasseriesgeorges.be.
This perennial favorite and quintessential brasserie near the Cambre Woods is always bustling under the din of chatty diners and clanging silverware. People come for the copious seafood platter, but there is plenty of other brasserie fare to choose from, as well as Belgian beers to wash it all down. On sunny days, make a beeline for the coveted tables on the terrace.

Toucan Brasserie
$$$ French
Avenue Louis Lepoutre 1, Ixelles. Tram 92: Ma Campagne. 02 345 30 17. www.toucanbrasserie.com.
Located between Place du Châtelain and Place Brugmann, this modern brasserie boasts both gorgeous décor and an eclectic menu specializing in Belgian and French classics with a modern twist. The restaurant has earned itself quite a reputation in the capital, so be sure to make reservations.

Via LaManna
$$$ Italian
Avenue Louise 233. Tram 94: Bailli. 02 626 16 00. www.vialamanna.com. Closed Sat & 2 weeks in Aug. No lunch Sun.
This "concept" complex on Avenue Louise resembles the Italian institution EATALY in Turin (and now in New York City), only on a smaller scale. While you'll find plenty of expensive dishes here, you can also drop into the Enoteca for a glass of wine and some tapas. No time to sit down? The on-site market has all the ingredients to create an Italian feast at home.

Vini Divini
$$$ Italian
Rue du Berger, 28, Ixelles. Metro: Porte de Namur. 047 726 14 87. www.vini-divini.be. Closed Sun. No dinner Mon–Wed. No lunch Sat.
No wider than a large hallway, this tiny Italian *ristorante* uses only the finest quality products. Food is prepared in a makeshift kitchen and the result is nothing short of miraculous, given the limited space. Shelves stacked with wines hover over the tables and the counter-style bar, the best place to watch the chef at work. Reservations are a must.

RESTAURANTS

East of Center

Mamy Louise
$$$ French
Avenue aux Cerisiers 212, Woluwé-St-Lambert. Metro: Gribaumon. 02 779 00 96. www.mamylouise.be. Closed Sun. No lunch Sat.
With its neutral hues and accent photos of New York City, Mamy Louise oozes casual sophistication, and serves a variety of Belgian dishes for lunch and dinner. *Boulettes-frites* (meatballs and fries) and *Stoemp* (mashed potatoes and sausage) share menu space with salads, pastas and a scrumptious tomato soup. Save room for the cheesecake with *speculaas* cookie crust.

Bon Bon
$$$$ French
Avenue de Tervuren 453, Woluwé-St-Pierre. Tram 44: Trois Couleurs. 02 346 66 15. www.bon-bon.be. Closed Sat & Sun.
One of Brussels' most gushed-over chefs, Christophe Hardiquest recently moved his restaurant from its Uccle location to this new leafy outpost in Woluwé-St-Pierre. The larger dining room here harbors the same refined service and market-fresh cuisine. For foodies with money, it's worth the splurge.

Antwerp

Caravan
$ Belgian
Damplein 17. 03 297 68 52.
A former apothecary forms the setting for this friendly, no-frills café, the place to come for weekend brunch as well as home-cooked meals. Nearby is North Railway Park (Park Spoor Noord), a new green space in Antwerp's trendy Het Eilandje neighborhood.

Salon de Thé Claude
$ French
Schelderstraat 79. 03 237 05 01. www.salondetheclaude.be. Lunch only. Closed Mon & Tue.
In a city that is distinctively Flemish and proud of it, it's rare to find French flair, but this tearoom and café is *la vie en rose* – Antwerp style. Come for breakfast or afternoon tea, and, *bien sur*, the quintessential Parisian confection – delicate buttercream-filled *macarons*.

Patine
$$ International
Leopold de Waelstraat 1. 03 257 09 19. wijnbistropatine.be.
Located in Antwerp's Zuid district, this unpretentious wine bar and café is tops for fresh and affordable sandwiches, pasta and quiche, even an empanada. In the evening, live music sessions pair perfectly with the generous wine list. Upstairs, a B&B with three rental apartments ranks among the city's best finds.

Dock's Café
$$$ French
Jordaenskaai 7. 03 226 63 30. www.docks.be. Closed Sun.
Despite the seafaring theme of the interior, Dock's menu is not limited to seafood platters and oysters – though those are top choices at this popular quayside brasserie. Here, Chef Yannick Frooninckx sources his produce and meat from a local farm and fashions flawless dishes. A lovely terrace and a set lunch menu (two courses for €15) make this café a must.

Het Gebaar

$$$$ Contemporary Belgian
Leopoldstraat 24. 03 232 37 10.
www.rogervandamme.com.
Lunch Only. Closed Sun & Mon.
For the most indulgent lunch
of your life, you won't be
disappointed at this phenomenal
restaurant located in the botanical
gardens in central Antwerp.
Chef Roger van Damme is fast
becoming one of the country's
most talked-about chefs.
His food is sublime and artistic,
inventive and alchemistic, visual
and seductive. Het Gebaar is as
good as it gets.

't Zilte

$$$$ Contemporary
Hanzestedenplaats 1. 03 283 40 40.
www.tzilte.be. Closed Sun.
Occupying the ninth floor of the
new Museum Aan de Stroom
(MAS), opened in May 2011, 't
Zilte is literally on top in the rust-
colored, stone and glass structure
that overlooks the Schelde River.
Pair a view over the city with
creative cuisine and it all adds up
to a meal to remember.

Bruges

Lotus

$ Vegetarian
Wapenmakerstraat 5. 050 33 10 78.
www.lotus-brugge.be. Lunch only.
Closed Sat & Sun.
An excellent value in pricey Bruges,
this vegetarian restaurant also has
a few carnivore options. The menu
may be limited, but tasty dishes
appeal with fresh and colorful
ingredients. Specials change daily,
and the location in the center of
Bruges is ideal.

Veal sweetbreads, Parkrestaurant

©Parkrestaurant

Parkrestaurant

$$$ Belgian
*Minderbroederstraat 1. 05 034
64 42. www.parkrestaurant.be.*
Closed Sun. No dinner Thu.
This friendly family-run restaurant,
housed in an elegant 1849
mansion, is the go-to special-
occasion spot in Bruges. Though
traditional Belgian and French
dishes reign in the chandelier-lit
dining room, the menu is anything
but old-fashioned. A four-course
dinner menu (the only option on
Saturday nights) will run you €40,
and a three-course lunch menu is
available for half that price.

Pro Deo

$$$ Belgian
Langestraat 161. 05 033 73 55.
www.restaurantprodeo.be.
*Closed Sun. No lunch Sat;
no dinner Mon.*
From filet mignon and shrimp
croquettes to spaghetti carbonara
and eel with cream sauce, there's
something for everyone at this
welcoming restaurant that
manages to be both close to all
things yet off the beaten tourist
track. The cozy dining room is
decorated in wood and warmth
but it's not big, so reserve ahead. .

RESTAURANTS

De Karmeliet

©De Karmeliet

De Karmeliet

$$$$ Contemporary

Langestraat 19. 05 033 82 59.
www.dekarmeliet.be. Closed Sun
& Mon.

Acclaimed chef Geert Van Hecke presides over the kitchen in this award-winning restaurant set in the historical heart of Bruges. Here, he strives for perfection in an array of thematic menus that highlight the best of the Low Country and the season. At De Karmeliet, gastronomes swoon over food that is as much a destination as the city of Bruges itself.

Den Dyver

$$$$ Belgian

Dijver 5. 05 033 60 69.
www.dyver.be. Closed Wed & Thu.

Solid traditional cuisine, well-marinated in Belgian beer, is the hallmark of this beloved eatery, whose menu is guaranteed to satisfy the heartiest appetites – beer lover or not. Housed in an 18C patrician residence and draped in tapestries, Den Dyver has won several Beer and Gastronomy awards. The three-course lunch menu will run you €24.

Visscherie

$$$$ Seafood

Vismarkt 8. 05 033 02 12.
www.visscherie.be. Closed Tue.

Visscherie reigns as the fish market on the fish market, and – you guessed it – fish is de rigueur here at Bruges' favorite ocean-faring table. At dinner, the à la carte menu swims with classic soups, crustaceans, and main courses, or you can put yourself in the chef's hands by choosing the set four-course tasting (€78).

Ghent

Fabula Rasa

$ Belgian

Ferdinand Lousbergkaai 134.
09 225 63 30. www.fabula-rasa.be.
No lunch Mon.

If tabula rasa means "blank slate," then Fabula Rasa must mean clean plate – and that's easy to do at this down-home brasserie. There's nothing fancy on the menu, just hearty, reasonably priced comfort food (steak *frites*, spaghetti Bolognese, croque monsieur) and daily specials on the chalkboard. Booking on weekends is advised.

MUST EAT

Julie's House

$ American

Kraanlei 13. 09 233 33 90. www.
julieshouse.be. Closed Mon & Tue.
Muffins and cakes and pies, oh my!
Everything here is baked with love
and served with joy by the owner.
Located next to the Gravensteen
Castle, this is the place to come for
afternoon tea, but folks also flip for
the delicious weekend breakfasts,
including eggs, croissants, and
American-style pancakes.

Julie's House

©Julie's House

Bij den Wijzen & den Zot

$$ Belgian

Hertogstraat 42. 09 223 42 30.
www.bijdenwijzenendenzot.be.
Closed Sun & Mon.
The first restaurant to open in
the ancient and quaint Patershol
neighborhood of Ghent, this
restaurant with the impossible-
to-pronounce name serves Ghent
specialties like waterzooi (a creamy
seafood stew) that originated
in this city.

De Blauwe Kiosk

$$ Seafood

Kouter 1. 09 328 79 71.
www.deblauwekiosk.be.
Lunch only. Closed Mon–Fri.
Set on one of Ghent's main squares,
the Kouter (the site of a Sunday
flower market), this unassuming

blue shack is where Ghent locals in
the know drop by for oysters and
white wine.

Le Baan Thai

$$ Thai

Corduwaniersstraat 57. 09 233 21
41. Dinner only (and Sun lunch).
Located in the ancient and trendy
Patershol neighborhood, this
restaurant hides in a courtyard, but
you can find it easily by following
the crowds. Typical Thai offerings
– spicy curries, spring rolls and
plenty of vegetarian options – are
on hand. Portions are large, so
bring some friends and share.
Reservations are essential.

Per Bacco

$$ Italian

Sint-Jacobsnieuwstraat 56.
09 324 83 32. www.perbacco.be.
Closed Mon & Tue.
In Italian, *per bacco* is an expression
of pleasure and surprise. Between
the Burata mozzarella, the hand-
made pasta and pesto, and the
impeccable desserts – including a
luscious limoncello cheesecake –
you may find yourself muttering
"per bacco" all through the evening.

Bord'eau

$$$$ Seafood

Sint-Veerleplein 5. 09 223 20 00.
www.oudevismijn.be.
No dinner Sun.
Housed in the old fish market,
opposite the Design Museum,
and set along the river Lys, this
newcomer on the culinary scene
(late 2010) is making a splash.
The mix of modern and old-world
architecture features a glass wall
that showcases the magnificent
city of Ghent, while the menu nets
scrumptious seafood.

RESTAURANTS

HOTELS

Brussels boasts a wide range of accommodations for every budget and comfort level. Though there are a few high-end hotels, concentrated near the Grand Place or Avenue Louise, most accommodations fall into the boutique-hotel category, which offer stylish rooms where visitors can experience a more intimate stay.

Between the European Parliament and the nearly 2,000 international corporations in Brussels, the city draws not only tourists, but also myriad business travelers. Thus many hotels, especially around the European Quarter, offer meeting facilities and business centers, and more apart-hotels are cropping up to accommodate longer stays. Expect a high service standard in most places, with a brigade of helpful English-speaking staff members eager to serve. Generally speaking, the high season for hotels is late spring and summer, and rates are lower in other months of the year.

Prices and Amenities

The accommodations described here are classified according to the price for a **double room** for one night, during high season, not including taxes or surcharges. Many hotels in Brussels will be more expensive during the week, and less on weekends. Hotels, especially around the European Quarter, have better rates in August, when Europeans typically take their vacation. Prices vary considerably depending on the season and time of year, so be sure to call beforehand to check the rates for the period chosen for your stay. Most hotels accept major credit cards and offer air-conditioning.

Online Booking

Rack rates (published rates) provided by hotels are usually higher than website deals. Online booking is therefore often cheaper, with promotional rates for early booking or prepayment. Hotels sometimes offer special packages and themed packages available directly through the hotel. Check out the following **websites** before you make a reservation:

Hotel Bloom

©Hotel Bloom

www.hotels.be – Database for Belgian hotels, searchable by price, location and amenities.

www.brussels-hotels.com – You can search this database by neighborhood and rating.

www.visitbrussels.be – The official website of the Tourism and Convention Bureau of Brussels has a hotel directory and an online booking service.

www.b-aparthotels.com – The specialist of long stays in Brussels has four B-Aparthotels properties in key locations around Brussels, and more than 150 apartments, studios and suites for rent.

$ under €100
$$ €100 to €175
$$$ €175 to €250
$$$$ over €250

Lower Town

🛌 Hotel Bloom
$ 305 rooms
Rue Royale 250. 02 220 66 11. www.hotelbloom.com.
It's spring every day at this hotel located near Le Botanique. Ten types of rooms, from large to extra-extra large, all have a white backdrop and Bloom-themed design elements done by a local artist. Business travelers appreciate the onsite meeting facilities and free Wi-Fi throughout the hotel. Parking is available for a fee.

Atlas Hotel
$$ 88 rooms
Rue due Vieux Marche aux Grains. 02 502 60 06. www.atlas.be.
In the heart of the Antoine Dansaert shopping area, and just steps from the bars and restaurants of Place St-Géry, this fine hotel

has all the makings for a great holiday in Brussels. Wi-Fi and tea and coffee come complimentary in each room, five of which are duplex rooms with kitchenettes.

Hotel Café Pacific
$$ 12 rooms
Rue Antoine Dansaert 57. 02 213 00 80. www.hotelcafepacific.com.
Through a narrow entrance off of the trendy Rue Antoine Dansaert, and close to the metro and sightseeing, this small boutique hotel supplies comfort and trend at affordable prices. Each room touts its own personality and offers modern touches like Wi-Fi and hairdryers. The hotel's Champagne and wine bar is a hip meeting spot.

Hotel Welcome
$$ 17 rooms
Quai au Bois à Brûler 3. 02 217 18 87. www.hotelwelcome.com.
A surprising value in downtown Brussels, this friendly hotel has rooms that tour the world in theme and décor. Breakfast and Wi-Fi are included in rates that are cheaper on the weekend.

Radisson Blu Royal Hotel
$$ 281 rooms
Rue du Fossé aux Loups 47. 02 219 28 28. www.radissonblue.com.
This luxurious hotel's magnificent Art Deco façade welcomes guests for a comfortable and stylish stay in the city center. Brussels' best attractions, including the Grand Place, are just minutes from the hotel's front door, and the popular **Belga Queen** *(see Must Eat)* restaurant is right down the street. The hotel boasts first-class amenities such as free wireless

Internet access and a fitness center and spa. The onsite **Sea Grill** *(see Must Eat)* is one of the most highly acclaimed in Brussels.

The Dominican Hotel
$$$ 150 rooms
Rue Léopold 9. 02 203 08 08.
www.dominican.be.
Location and style blend at this hotel, which occupies the former site of a 15C Dominican Abbey. Situated just behind the La Monnaie theater, the Dominican puts Brussels at guests' doorstep. Chic in a palette of warm hues, rooms feature comforts like Nespresso coffee, bathrobes and slippers, and complimentary Wi-Fi. The downstairs bar is a popular spot for a nightcap.

Le Méridien
$$$ 224 rooms
Carrefour de l'Europe 3.
02 548 42 11. www.lemeridian-
brussels.com.
Elegant guest rooms and suites offer a sanctuary of unmatched comfort in the heart of the city. Easily accessible, opposite the Gare Centrale(central train station), Le Méridien is walking distance away from the Grand Place and other Brussels attractions. Take your pick between work and play: you'll find both a business center and fitness facilities here.

NH du Grand Sablon
$$$ 196 rooms
Rue Bodenbroek 2–4. 02 512 67 66.
www.nh-hotels.com.
This member of the NH chain reigns over one of the most beautiful squares in Brussels, the Place du Grand Sablon, which is lined with shops, restaurants and cafés. With easy access to museums, parks and the Sablon's weekend antiques market, the NH is one of the best-situated hotels in Brussels.

Royal Windsor Hotel Grand Place
$$$ 266 rooms
Rue Duquesnoy 5–7. 02 515 55 55.
www.royalwindsorbrussels.com.
Whether traveling for business or pleasure, guests here are treated to a blend of tradition and sophistication, with rooms and suites in subdued and sensual color palettes. The Royal Windsor boasts a perfect location, just off the Grand Place. It's steps from

Terrace of the Royal Windsor Hotel

©Royal Windsor Hotel Grand Place

SQUARE, a.k.a. the Congress Center, and walking distance from the Gare Centrale, should you decide to take a train excursion during your stay.

🏨 Hotel Amigo
$$$$ 173 rooms
Rue de l'Amigo 1–3. 02 547 47 47. www.hotelamigo.com.
This converted 16C prison is one you'll never want to escape; it now ranks among the finest luxury hotels in Brussels, located steps from the Grand Place. Rooms are traditional yet modern, with rich touches like embroidered fabrics and Flemish tapestries, as well as the latest technology. Magritte prints decorate the bedrooms and Hergé's lovable Tintin animates the marble baths, while top-floor suites have great views of Lower Town. It's hard to resist the sumptuous décor, the martini bar and restaurant, and the impeccable service here.

🏨 Hotel Metropole
$$$$ 305 rooms
Place de Brouckère 31. 02 217 23 00. www.metropolehotel.com.
This sumptuous palace dating from 1895 is the city's only 19C property still open for business. Catering to the seasoned traveler looking for elegance and refinement, the Art Deco-style lodging also offers gourmet restaurants, a fitness center and event rooms to add to its appeal.

Le Dixseptieme
$$$$ 24 rooms
Rue de la Madeleine 25. 02 502 17 17. www.ledixseptieme.be.
Close to the Grand Place and the main train station, this elegant hotel occupies what was once

Le Dixseptieme
©Hotel Le Dixseptieme

the residence of the 17C Spanish Ambassador. Finely decorated and spacious, each room invites you to indulge a little in Brussels. Three intimate meeting rooms are also part of the package.

Upper Town

Aqua Hotel
$$ 97 rooms
Rue de Stassart 43. 02 213 01 01. www.aqua-hotel-brussels.com.
Close to the historic center, the European institutions, and Avenue Louise for tony shopping, this newcomer combines trendy design with the comforts of a first-class lodging. High above the lobby, a unique art installation from the studio Arne Quinze is the focal point, but the fitness room and free Internet access are also a plus.

Hotel Eurostars Montgomery
$$ 63 rooms
Avenue de Tervuren 134. 02 741 85 11. www.eurostars montgomery.com.
Removed from the city center, but just a few metro stops away, this property exudes the ambience of an old English gentlemen's club. It appeals to business travelers or vacationers who wish to hide out from the scramble of downtown.

HOTELS

145

Martin's Central Park

©Martin's Central Park

Themed rooms display either a traditional, a romantic or an Asian décor, and five private meeting rooms adapt to most any event.

Martin's Central Park
$$ 100 rooms
Boulevard Charlemagne 80. 02 230 85 55. www.martins centralpark.com.
Designed to meet all the high-tech needs of demanding businessmen, yet also a perfect base for a weekend spent discovering Brussels, the well-appointed rooms in this European Quarter hotel come with a renovated bathroom, air-conditioning, Internet connection, a desk and a flat-screen TV. Icones bar and restaurant makes a nice place to get a bite to eat or chill out with a cocktail at the end of the day.

Marriott Executive Apartments Brussels
$$-$$$ 56 suites
Rue du Parnasse 15. 02 505 29 29. www.marriott.com.
The ideal solution when international travel takes you away from home for longer periods of time, these one- and two-bedroom executive apartments are fully equipped with kitchen facilities, Internet access, on-site parking

and access to the fitness center next door at the Renaissance Hotel. It's a short walk to the European institutions, Place du Luxembourg, and metro stops.

Aloft
$$$ 147 rooms
Place Jean Rey 1. 02 800 08 08. www.aloftbrussels.com.
Opened in September 2010, Aloft, a vision of W hotels group, is a stylish and modern newcomer in the European Quarter, with open and airy loft-like rooms and common spaces. A grab-and-go café, a trendy bar, and hotel-wide free Wi-Fi number among the amenities. Go in August when rates hit rock bottom.

Renaissance
$$$ 262 rooms
Rue du Parnasse 19. 02 505 29 29. www.renaissancehotels.com.
The hotel has been fully refurbished and is conveniently situated just a stone's throw from Place du Luxembourg, with its lively bar and restaurant scene. Comfortable beds and a friendly staff are high points, along with an indoor heated pool and fitness center. Note that you'll have to pay for Wi-Fi access here, even in the lobby.

Sofitel Brussels Le Louise
$$$ 169 rooms
Avenue de la Toison d'Or 40.
02 514 22 00. www.sofitel.com.
Fully refurbished in 2008, this member of the Sofitel chain is located between the exclusive shops of Avenue Louise and the sights of downtown. All rooms are tastefully furnished and equipped with Sofitel's "MyBed" to assure you a good night's sleep. The Crystal Lounge and its outdoor terrace are popular meet-and-greet spots, but 24-hour room service is also available, should you prefer to relax in your room.

North of Center

Frederiksborg
$ 30 rooms
Avenue Broustin 118, Koekelberg.
02 425 14 22. www.frederiksborg.be.
Located facing the impressive Bailica of the Sacred Heart, this budget inn has 30 small rooms, plus free Internet. The on-site restaurant serves French and Danish cuisine with set-menu options, and the tavern offers continental and English breakfasts, as well as afternoon tea and snacks. The nearest metro stop is a 15-minute walk away.

Husa President Park
$ 297 rooms
Boulevard du Roi Albert II 44,
Schaerbeek. 02 203 20 20.
www.husapresidentpark.com.
Four styles of accommodations, from standard rooms to junior suites, are tastefully decorated, spacious and light, reflecting the welcoming atmosphere of the hotel. Each room is well equipped with Wi-Fi access, hair dryers, TV

and air-conditioning. The location, near the Gare du Nord (north train station), means that Brussels and the nearby Expo Center are easily accessible. If you want to go for broke, the Presidential Suite has its own kitchen.

Holiday Inn Garden Court Brussels Expo
$$ 79 rooms
Avenue de l'Imperatrice
Charlotte 6, Heysel. 02 478 70 80.
www.holiday-inn.com./bru-expo.
This simple hotel enjoys a prime location within walking distance of Brussels Expo, as well as the Atomium and Bruparck. It's also close to the Royal Domain, with its greenhouses, castle, and eye-catching Japanese Tower and Chinese Pavilion. The nearby metro line will take you to the city center.

Ibis Brussels Expo-Atomium
$$ 81 rooms
Chaussée Romaine 572, Heysel.
02 461 00 21. www.ibishotel.com.
Located 8km/5mi from the city center, and conveniently situated opposite the main entrance of the exhibition center (Brussels Expo), the Ibis is well-suited to hosting business travelers, as well as families visiting the nearby Atomium and the attractions at Bruparck. Clean lines mark the comfortable rooms.

Sheraton Brussels Hotel
$$ 511 rooms
Place Rogier 3, St-Josse. 02 224 31
11. www.sheraton.com./brussels.
Rising high above the Brussels skyline, the Sheraton sits at the core of the city's business district, and just a few minutes' stroll from Brussels' main shopping area, Rue

Neuve. The hotel is situated on the Brussels Little Ring Road, with direct metro access right in front. Aside from the comfy beds, the highlight here is the 30th-floor fitness center, sauna, and rooftop swimming pool, with Brussels as its impressive backdrop.

Thon Hotel City Centre
$$ 454 rooms
Avenue du Boulevard 17, St-Josse. 02 205 15 11. www.thonhotel-city center.com.
This welcoming hotel boasts smart, well-appointed rooms and a range of amenities, including a choice of 40 international TV channels, pay-movies, and tea- and coffee-making facilities. The 29th-floor relaxation center has a fitness room, sun beds, and a sauna with panoramic views across Brussels. The hotel is just a short walk from the cultural hotspot Le Botanique and the pedestrian shopping street Rue Neuve.

South of Center

🛏 Le Châtelain
$$ 107 rooms
Rue du Châtelain 17. 02 646 00 55. www.le-chatelain.com.
European hotel rooms are known to be notoriously small, but this hotel belies that fact with some of the largest hotel rooms in the city. Take your pick between superior rooms, executive rooms, junior suites and ambassador suites, all outfitted with the luxuries of home. The location in a neighborhood teeming with bars and restaurants can't be beat.

Vintage Hotel
$$ 29 rooms
De Joncker 45. 02 533 99 80. www.vintagehotel.be.
Contemporary vintage may seem like an oxymoron, but this hotel blends both seamlessly. Rooms are accented with furnishings from the past century, yet still touched by modern amenities like Internet access and TV. The metro station is just a two-minute walk from the front door, as is the chic shopping along Avenue Louise. Weather permitting, the lovely garden terrace is a tranquil perch to enjoy a glass of wine.

White Hotel
$$ 53 rooms
Avenue Louise 212. 02 644 29 29. www.thewhitehotel.be.
This hotel's palette is all about white, but a stay here is certain to add a splash of color to your Brussels visit. On the fashionable Avenue Louise, the White Hotel features installations and exhibits by local Belgian designers. Guestrooms have flat-panel TVs as well as complimentary wireless Internet access. You can rent bikes onsite too.

🛏 Odette en Ville
$$$ 8 rooms
Rue du Châtelain 25. 02 640 26 26. www.chez-odette.com.
Set in a restored town house in a neighborhood near Place du Châtelain, this elegant establishment riffs on old Hollywood glamour. Modern yet classic, in hues of black and taupe, the rooms and common areas offer both comfort and sophistication. Read in the library off the lobby or sip Champagne in the candlelit bar.

Odette en Ville

©Bluecic.com/G.Miclotte/Odette En Ville

Plenty of restaurants and shopping venues lie within walking distance.

The Pantone Hotel
$$$ 61 rooms
Place Loix 1 St-Gilles. 02 541 48 98.
www.pantonehotel.com.
In often-gray Brussels, this colorful boutique hotel, brought to you by the folks that invented the Pantone Matching System® of printing colors, livens up your stay with quiet rooms in the trendy St-Gilles neighborhood. Each room sports its own vibrant hue, along with flat-screen TVs, designer touches, and photography by local artist Victor Levy.

Conrad Hotel
$$$$ 269 rooms
Avenue Louise 71. 02 542 42 42.
www.conradhotels.com.
Synonymous with luxury, the Conrad boasts exceptional accommodations in sophisticated surroundings. Each room wraps guests in sumptuous appointments. Here you'll find the Aspria Wellness Center (*see* SPAS), with dozens of treatments and an indoor pool. Tourist attractions, metro stations and

some of Brussels' most vibrant neighborhoods are within easy striking distance.

Manos Premier
$$$$ 50 rooms
Chaussée de Charleroi 100–104.
02 537 96 82. www.manos
premier.com.
A closely guarded secret, this tony property near Avenue Louise is both intimate and luxurious, giving travelers the feeling of being pampered in a private home. Rooms are done with Louis XV and XVI furnishings and marble baths, while downstairs, Kolya restaurant serves refined cuisine under a glass roof. The back garden offers a haven of peace amid the bustle of Brussels.

East of Center

La Tour de Bebelle
$ 3 rooms
Rue St-Hubert 44, Woluwé-St-Pierre. 02 762 72 55.
www.latourdebebelle.be.
For a quiet stay in Brussels with all the comforts of home, yet still close enough to enjoy the city's fabulous attractions, this B&B in

HOTELS

Woluwé-St-Pierre can't be beat. Each of the three rooms, named for Belgian artists, is warm and inviting, with quality bedding. Breakfast is included in the rate, and guests have access to a microwave and a refrigerator.

West of Center

be Manos
$$$ 60 rooms
Square de l'aviation 23–27, Anderlecht. 02 520 65 65. www.bemanos.com.
The Poulgouras family, who own three other Manos hotels in Brussels, are known for turning old town houses into magnificent sanctuaries. And they've done it again at be Manos – their first boutique hotel. Contemporary design pops with conviviality and comfort, and the third-floor bar and terrace has become a lively hotspot for night owls. Rooms use space wisely and don't miss a beat when it comes to modern comforts.

Antwerp

Patine
$ 2 rooms
Leopold de Waelstraat 1. 03 257 09 19. wijnbistropatine.be.
This cozy wine bar/restaurant/inn nods to pubs that doubled as guesthouses for weary travelers in the past. Upstairs, a large studio and a three-bedroom apartment, each with a kitchen, are ideal for families or extended stays. Breakfast is included in the price, and weekly rates are available.

Sir Plantin Hotel
$ 176 rooms
Plantin en Moretuslei 136. 03 271 07 00. www.sirplantin-antwerp.com.
The perfect location for an excursion from Brussels, this contemporary hotel in the Zurenborg – Antwerp's vibrant Art Nouveau district – is decked out with designer touches. Convenient to the Gare Centrale and only 2km/1.2mi from the historic center, the hotel boasts stylish rooms, including some with connecting doors for families. There is a casual restaurant and bar onsite, as well as a complimentary in-room minibar.

Sir Plantin Hotel
©Sir Plantin Hotel

Hotel O Antwerp
$$ 14 rooms.
Leopold de Waelplaats 34. 03 292 65 10. www.hotelhotelo.be.
This boutique property, brand new on Antwerp's pillow scene, features spacious rooms and two spa suites – complete with outdoor whirlpool and sauna – to maximize your comfort. All the rooms are done with a mix of classic and vintage furniture, and each has a view over the square and the Fine Arts Museum, in the popular Zuid (south) neighborhood of the city. Guests will find an iPad on every floor for their use.

MUST STAY

Hotel Prinse
$$ 35 rooms
Keizerstraat 63. 03 226 40 50.
www.hotelprinse.be.
Guests are welcomed into the
Prinse via the quiet courtyard and
garden of a 16C mansion. Besides
rooms decked out with clean lines
and neutral tones, all the modern
conveniences one expects from
a sophisticated hotel in stylish
Antwerp are here: Wi-Fi, flat-screen
TVs, and private parking.

Radisson Blu Park Lane
$$ 174 rooms
Van Eycklei 34. 03 285 85 85.
www.radisson.com.
Set at the edge of Antwerp's
diamond district, just opposite the
triangular city park, the Radisson
Blu Park Lane puts the main
shopping streets and the historic
center within easy reach. Rooms,
some with views of the park, are
modern and sophisticated, with
free Internet access in each.
When it's time to relax, take a dip
in the indoor pool or indulge in a
Turkish steam bath.

Hotel De Witte Lelie
$$$ 10 rooms
Keizerstraat 16–18. 03 226 19 66.
dewittelelie.be.
Located in three renovated 17C
gabled mansions, and perfectly
situated between the Meir and
the Het Eilandje neighborhoods,
this glamorous boutique property
has only ten rooms, each with an
ensuite bath stocked with Hermès
products. Flower-filled common
areas blend contemporary and
antique styles, and the menu of
personal services is designed
to pamper.

Hotel De Witte Lelie

©Hotel De Witte Lelie

Bruges

Hotel Adornes
$$ 20 rooms
Sint-Annarei 26. 05 034 13 36.
www.adornes.be.
You'll feel right at home in this
Bruges mansion, which boasts
serene canal views in a quiet part
of the city – only a 10-minute
walk from the center. Guests here
love the buffet breakfast as well
as having bicycles available to
ride around the city. Simple and
comfortable, rooms have twin or
double beds; some are even able
to accommodate families. Free Wi-
Fi is available in all of the hotel's
common areas.

Golden Tulip Hotel de Medici
$$$ 101 rooms
Potterierei 15. 050 33 98 33.
www.hoteldemedici.com.
Set on the canal, this hotel makes
the perfect *pied-a-terre* from
which to explore one of Belgium's
most beautiful cities. It's only a
10-minute walk to the market
square, and all the world class
museums that Bruges offers.
Spacious rooms are equipped
with the usual lineup of amenities,
including coffee and tea and
air-conditioning. Ten of the rooms
have connecting doors for families.

HOTELS

Hotel de Orangerie

$$$ 20 rooms

Kartuizerinnenstraat 10. 05 034 16 49. www.hotelorangerie.com.

One of the finest hotels in town is this 15C former convent, overlooking the picturesque Den Dijver Canal. The elegant haven exudes an old-world air with its paintings, silk-lined curtains and antiques. Nothing has been sacrificed when it comes to comfort and service. In winter, English afternoon tea is served in the cozy lounge by the open fire; in summer, tea can be taken on the terrace by the canal.

Hotel Die Swaene

$$$ 30 rooms

Steenhouwersdijk 1. 05 034 27 98. www.dieswaene-hotel.com.

The moment you step through the doors of the Hotel Die Swaene, you know you've entered a superb hotel in a magical city. This 15C mansion flanks one of the most beautiful canals in Bruges, within an easy walk of museums and restaurants. Individually decorated rooms are beautifully appointed with modern touches. Check out the new wing, the Canal House, which has eight rooms and two suites at water level, and a sunny terrace from which to enjoy the lovely view.

Hotel Egmond

$$$ 8 rooms

Minnewater 15. 05 034 14 45. www.egmond.be.

Located next to the Minne-waterpark – a.k.a. "the lake of love" – and enclosed in its own private garden, this 18C manor house feels like a piece of the English countryside. Period furnishings, open fireplaces and a beamed ceiling give you the idea. All the city's main historic attractions lie within easy walking distance of the hotel, and the Béguinage of Bruges is just around the corner. Room rates include breakfast, and parking is available for an added fee.

Relais Ravestein

$$$$ 16 rooms

Molenmeers 11. 05 047 69 47. www.relaisravestein.be.

The 16 suites in this canal-side hotel feature a minimalist design accented with luxurious touches, such as in-room Jacuzzis and flat-screen TVs. A marvelous place to sip coffee and watch the boats go by, the outdoor terrace is also a perfect perch for a cocktail. A central location and an on-site brasserie and bar are just a few more reasons to stay here.

Ghent

The Boatel

$$ 7 rooms

Voorhoutkaai 44. 09 267 10 30. www.theboatel.com.

For something different in traditional Ghent, take to the canals and stay on this boat, aptly named The Boatel. This barge has been retrofitted with five standard rooms below deck, and two bigger, more luxurious rooms on the upper deck. All rooms have TV, Internet access, showers and phone – but you'll have to rely on water breezes for air-conditioning.

Ghent River Hotel

$$ 77 rooms

Waaistraat 5. 09 266 10 10. www.ghent-river-hotel.be.

Both historic and modern, the Ghent River Hotel sits on the banks of the Leie River, in two historic buildings that once held a rice mill and a sugar refinery. Thanks to the ancient pier, the hotel is also accessible by boat. Exposed beams and brick walls lend an urban-chic feel, yet none of the property's historic charm has been lost. Besides modern, well decorated rooms, the hotel offers a cozy bar, a fitness room and sauna, and bike rentals.

Hotel Verhaegen
$$$ 4 rooms
Oude Houtlei 110. 09 265 07 60.
www.hotelverhaegen.be.
This 18C mansion, whose previous tenant list reads like a who's-who, is now a pristine B&B in the heart of historic Ghent, just a five-minute walk from the Graslei, the best-known quai of the medieval port. Interior designers, the owners have blended architectural heritage and modern comforts, with attention to even the smallest details in the individually decorated rooms. Have breakfast in your room, or in the quiet garden; in the evening, enjoy a nightcap by the fireplace.

Garden of Hotel Verhaegen
©Hotel Verhaegen

Marriott Ghent
$$$ 150 rooms
Drabstraat. 09 233 93 93.
www.marriott.com.
Overlooking the Korenlei, on the banks of the river Lys canal, this Marriott puts the best of Ghent at your feet and styles a modern interior in a historic building. The lobby bar, set under a glass dome, makes a pretty setting for an evening cocktail, while three restaurants will spoil you for choice. At night, the lights of Ghent's gabled canal-side houses reflect in the water to magical effect.

NH Gent Belfort
$$$ 174 rooms
Hoogpoort 63. 09 233 33 31.
www.nh-hotels.com.
A hidden treasure tucked away in the heart of Ghent, this unusual building stands in the shadow of the Town Hall. All of Ghent's attractions and shopping streets are within walking distance of the hotel. Contemporary rooms make a comfy place to hang out when you're not eating in the hotel's restaurant, working out in the fitness room, or enjoying a cocktail at the bar.

Hotel Gravensteen
$$$$ 49 rooms
Jan Breydelstraat 35. 09 225 11 50.
www.gravensteen.be.
Beginning in the lobby with its ornate moldings and wrought-iron chandeliers, this stunning hotel set in a 19C mansion shows off impeccable style and understated elegance. You'll feel like royalty here, next door to the entrance of the Castle of the Counts.

HOTELS

BRUSSELS

INDEX

List of Maps

INDEX